After the Internet

Dedicated to Levi Felix (1984–2017)

After the Internet

Ramesh Srinivasan
& Adam Fish

polity

First published in 2017 by Polity Press

Polity Press
65 Bridge Street
Cambridge CB2 1UR, UK

Polity Press
101 Station Landing
Suite 300
Medford, MA 02155
USA

ISBN-13: 978-1-5095-0617-0
ISBN-13: 978-1-5095-0618-7 (pb)

A catalogue record for this book is available from the British Library.

Library of Congress Cataloging-in-Publication Data

Names: Srinivasan, Ramesh, author. | Fish, Adam, author.
Title: After the Internet / Ramesh Srinivasan, Adam Fish.
Description: Cambridge, UK ; Malden, MA : Polity Press, 2017. | Includes
    bibliographical references and index.
Identifiers: LCCN 2017009318 (print) | LCCN 2017026160 (ebook) |
    ISBN 9781509506200 (Mobi) | ISBN 9781509506217 (Epub) | ISBN
    9781509506170 (hardback) | ISBN 9781509506187 (pbk.)
Subjects: LCSH: Internet–Social aspects. | Internet–Economic aspects.
Classification: LCC HM851 (ebook) | LCC HM851 .S725 2017 (print) |
    DDC 302.23/1–dc23
LC record available at https://lccn.loc.gov/2017009318

Typeset in 10.5 on 12 pt Sabon by Toppan Best-set Premedia Limited
Printed and bound in the United Kingdom by Clays Ltd, St Ives PLC.

For further information on Polity, visit our website: politybooks.com

Contents

List of Figures	*vi*
Acknowledgments	*vii*
Introduction: After the Internet	1
1 Reimagining Technology with Global Communities	25
2 Hacking the Hacktivists	48
3 Media Activism: Shaping Online and Offline Networks	73
4 After the Cloud: Do Silk Roads Lead to Data Havens?	103
Coda	*130*
References	*135*
Index	*157*

List of Figures

1.1 Interface of the Tribal Peace Native
American system   36

1.2 The first version of a fluid ontology created
with tribal communities across San
Diego County   38

1.3 Zuni leadership examining an indigenous map   40

1.4 Zuni community members collectively viewing
digital objects via *Amidolanne*   42

2.1 Higinio O. Ochoa III's selfie-incrimination   60

2.2 Ross Ulbricht's LinkedIn page   61

2.3 GCHQ's JTRIG computer network
attacks (CNA)   68

3.1 Social media revolution t-shirt   74

3.2 The Tweet-Nadwa (or "Tweet up") bringing
activists together with real-time conversations
online in Cairo, June 2011   85

3.3 Mosireen space   88

3.4 Tahrir Cinema   92

3.5 Military helicopter dropping flags on protesters
in Cairo's Tahrir Square, early July 2013   97

4.1 NSA's New Collection Posture   105

4.2 NSA Data Center in Utah   106

4.3 The house in Reykjavik where
WikiLeaks worked   117

Acknowledgments

Ramesh is truly grateful to his dear friend and conspirator Adam Fish for the inspiration to work together to fight for an internet in line with principles of democracy and social justice. This book marks but the latest in nearly a dozen years of collaboration. It could not have been written by either of us alone but comes from the union of the authors and exceeds the sum of each of us individually.

Ramesh thanks his sublime partner Syama for all her support in helping him dedicate himself to making this book possible. He also is truly grateful for the presence, love, and care of his parents Seenu and Sita and brother Mahesh. He thanks his incredible informants from across the world who have taught him the power of fighting for community sovereignty, equality, and a more ethical world. He thanks the National Science Foundation, UCLA, the Southern California Tribal Chairmen's Association, the A:shiwi A:wan Museum and Heritage Center, Rhizomatica, and the inspiring figures, particularly from the Mosireen collective, with whom he broke bread over three years in the midst of Tahrir Square and its transformations.

Adam thanks Ramesh for a decade of collaborative creative work and play. Lucas Follis deserves thanks for sharing his wisdom and generating many ideas around hacktivism. Ideas for chapter 2 were first explored in discussions with him and resulted in A. Fish & L. Follis, "Edgework, State Power, and

Hacktivists," *HAU: Journal of Ethnographic Theory*, 5(2) (2015): 383–90 and A. Fish & L. Follis, "Gagged and Doxed: Hacktivism's Self-Incrimination Complex," *International Journal of Communication*, 10 (2016): 3281–300.

The research in Iceland was funded by the European Cooperation in Science and Technology, COST Action IS1202; Security Lancaster; the Faculty of Arts and Social Sciences at Lancaster University; and the Department of Sociology at the University of Lancaster. Thanks go out to the University of Iceland for their generous visiting professorship in the summer of 2015. Alex Johnson should be thanked for her help in finding pirates and data centers in Iceland. Adam thanks his wife Robin for her love, support, and endurance, and his daughter Io for providing play and comic relief.

Together, we dedicate this book to the memory of our inspiring friend and brother Levi Felix, a visionary in his life. His work focused on creating greater mindful awareness in our interactions with technology remains a guiding light for us both.

Introduction:
After the Internet

> We are creating a world where anyone, anywhere may express his or her beliefs, no matter how singular, without fear of being coerced into silence or conformity.

> (Barlow 1996)

In his bold declaration of the independence of cyberspace, John Perry Barlow, founder of the Electronic Frontier Foundation and a well-known figure in internet counterculture circles, proudly announced that networked technology would bring the world together as a singular and "free" space. His words, quoted above, speak to optimistic and aspirational principles that imagine the internet as autonomous from control, surveillance, and manipulation. This reflects an ideology that prioritizes individual liberty over the practices of the state or society.

These words from Barlow represent an important philosophy by which the internet has been imagined and described. Yet now, over 20 years since Barlow's declaration, the internet and what it stands for remains contested. Commercial, governmental, public, and activist interests are in conflict and dialogue as we think about the future of the internet.

We have long heard about the democratic promise of the internet. As a decentralized network, the internet would empower its users equally. It would evade the top-down political economies of corporations that have monopolized older media networks of television and radio. It could embolden citizens to share their stories, design different sites, and mobilize and network from the grassroots. It would transform our world into a "global village" (Srinivasan 2017). Yet whose global village are we speaking about? And has such a global village of equality come to be?

There remains both considerable support for and critique of Barlow's claims. Several writers use his words as an example of the libertarian ideology present in technoliberal culture (Fish 2017b), explaining that Barlow mistakenly treats technology as autonomous and transcendent. Indeed, in a recent interview with *Wired* magazine noting the anniversary of the declaration, Barlow revealed that he still firmly believes in what he wrote in the 1996 document – that cyberspace is "naturally immune to sovereignty" and always will be (Greenberg 2016). In this sense, he treats the internet as *deterritorialized* (Deleuze & Guattari 1983), as existing above and beyond laws, contexts, places, and peoples.

Many dispute this, however. Andy Greenberg (2016), for example, provides a variety of examples that serve to discredit Barlow's claim. Greenberg notes recent political speeches, such as one from former French president Nicholas Sarkozy in 2013, that argue for the need to increase internet governance. Greenberg also notes the internet's dependency on a range of other infrastructures. Thus, from this perspective, one cannot cleanly disentangle the internet from related social, political, and cultural factors.

Andres Guadamuz (2016) builds on Greenberg's observation by citing the problematic "digital dualism" (Jurgenson 2012) that is inherent in Barlow's declaration. There is a mistaken duality between the digital and physical worlds that fails to recognize how they shape one another, he argues. Additionally, Guadamuz points to two other major flaws with the declaration: its exclusion of non-governmental forms of regulation and its Western-centric focus. That said, Guadamuz praises Barlow's declaration as a type of aspiration, highlighting the need to develop technologies and infrastructures that can overcome the corruption of existing political institutions that threaten human rights and free speech.

Further challenging Barlow's assertions of autonomy in cyberspace, Woody Evans (2016) notes the presence of internet governance institutions such as the International Corporation for Assigned Names and Numbers (ICANN) and the World-wide Web Consortium (W3C). Their existence is evidence that the internet is in fact centralized and hierarchical, despite being lauded as the opposite. Evans' main argument centers on refuting the essentialism of cyberspace that Barlow encourages. The internet therefore cannot be treated independently of cultural, social, and political practices.

Jessica Beyer and Fenwick McKelvey (2015) offer a different perspective on Barlow's 1996 claims. Their focus is on grassroots practices that are supported by networked digital technologies, like the internet. They present a number of examples that support Barlow's belief that cyberspace offers particular advantages for combating and resisting government regulation and intervention. Through a detailed discussion of the historical significance and trajectory of projects like Napster, BitTorrent, and MojoNation, the authors present digital piracy as a symbol of non-hierarchical organization and resistance to state power. In broad alignment with Barlow's current claims as expressed in the 2016 *Wired* interview, Beyer and McKelvey ultimately endorse these examples – even despite some of their failures – because of their capacity to undermine state power and control. Thus, even if governance institutions do attempt to control the internet, activists, hackers, and the public can weaken these through their subversive practices.

We share these different perspectives around Barlow's declaration to explain how contested the internet and what it signifies actually is. In a rhetorical and playful move, we thus title this book *After the Internet* with the intention of inspiring fellow scholars, activists, and the public to think of what our world may look like outside of its existing attachment to the internet "as is." To think "after the internet" (with a lower-case "i") is to stay mindful of the ideological baggage with which the internet is so often entangled.

We are concerned with how the political, economic, and ideological visions of the internet are controlled by Western corporate giants such as Google, Facebook, and Microsoft. These corporations not only increasingly dominate our software, hardware, and online practices, but they also increasingly control the "back end" by which user data is stored or communicated. This book thus examines existing critical theories, practices, and case studies to imagine a democratic internet where human rights, diversity, and social justice are respected and empowered.

Is the Internet Shit?

> The internet is shit today. It's broken. It was probably always broken, but it's worse than ever.
>
> (Sunde 2015)

These words, uttered by Peter Sunde, free software activist and one of the founders of the Pirate Bay sharing platform, speak to a negativity voiced by those concerned with the control of the internet by corporate and governmental institutions. Decades after the invention of the laptop, described by Bill Gates as "the most empowering tool we've ever created" (Grossman 2004), many critics have lamented how the internet has become intertwined with an economic system of neoliberal globalization marked by the "speeding up of time and shrinking of space" (Harvey 1990: 241).

We recognize ample scholarship that has problematized numerous social, economic, political, and cultural issues in relation to today's internet, all importantly noting that it is not the "internet" that should be the aim of such critique but the social, economic, and political forces that drive its deployment and application.

Concerns have surfaced around a number of core political and economic issues in relation to the internet. Across this book's chapters we share academic and journalistic research and analysis that relate the internet to surveillance, economic development, activism, and cultural diversity. We discuss research around surveillance that reveals that the internet is no longer a space for decentralized communication but instead capitalized upon by those who can best manage and manipulate digital infrastructures. It also begs the question as to why many no longer feel safe with public forms of digital expression without fear of persecution. We also share research focused on how the digital divide is a conceptually obsolete theme. Numerous studies have begun to show that blind access to technology does not in itself combat marginalization. Indeed, the myth of the internet as making people equal across the world and overcoming geographical inequality has been rebutted by sobering realities that show how digital economies bring disproportionate wealth to the limited few (Hargittai & Hsieh 2013). Further, we share research around technology and activism that reveals that the passive political use of social media, sometimes referred to as "slacktivism," is neither necessary nor sufficient to drive the waves of social movements that have taken hold of our world since late 2010. Finally, we also share research that has debunked the myth of the internet as a solution to the world's increased loss of bio-, linguistic, and cultural diversity. We argue that one cannot collect or preserve diversity merely by placing information online, nor can one ignore the environmentally damaging infrastructures that underpin digital communications, such as the electrical grid, the undersea fiber-optic cable system, or the industrial factory systems that assemble and produce network technologies as well as house our data.

We elaborate further on each of these major themes below.

Surveillance and Freedom

Perhaps the most publicly visible concern associated with the internet today relates to surveillance. It has raised fears that we have entered a "post-privacy" world without our consent. Not only is personal privacy of concern, but so also is our faith in acting publicly without fear of repression or repercussion. The revelations associated with the National Security Agency's (NSA) PRISM project, made public by whistleblower Edward Snowden, are staggering. Not only have major technology corporations been found to be complicit with state surveillance in a post-9/11 world, but we have also learned how data that technology users assumed to be private have instead fueled surveillance and control. When President Barack

Obama attempted to defend this effort, with an argument that the NSA gathered metadata rather than data, it reflected a clear attempt to obfuscate how powerful such forms of harvesting really are (Mayer 2013). When corporations and states can control and monitor where, when, and how technology is used, they can deem users as targets to be monitored and thereby circumvent *habeas corpus*.

WikiLeaks editor Julian Assange has made the point that both Google and the NSA are in the same business of collecting all information. While one organization sells this information to advertisers and the other monitors it for suspicious behavior, the goal for both is the same, to "collect it all," as one of the NSA's leaked documents makes abundantly clear (Greenwald 2014: 97). Such control of information allows states and corporations in partnership to "discipline" their citizens.

Science and technology scholar Laura DeNardis (2012) notes the role of the internet in creating this new form of disciplining, through what she terms "internet governance." DeNardis describes three key elements that have given rise to these dynamics: (1) the digital sphere as a place of political action; (2) the deployment of technology to negotiate terms of content control; and (3) the control of content through the use of private, hidden, and proprietary intermediaries. Her work demonstrates "how the technical arrangements of Internet governance inherently embed social and economic interests and, furthermore, how these arrangements can be co-opted to enact social control and content governance" (DeNardis 2012: 734).

Karine Nahon's (2014) work continues on this thread, exposing the substantial increase in state and self-regulation of the internet and posing the question of whether all mediation might eventually represent a form of opaque censorship, far removed from the gaze of distant users. Nahon discusses the power of the mediators in networked information, and the increased role of regulation in relation to that power.

The surveillance "issue" seems to have become a point of concern among technology users worldwide, and speaks to what philosophers Gilles Deleuze and Félix Guattari have derisively described as "State philosophy," or social formations and epistemologies that support the hierarchical and representational systems owned and managed by those in power (Massumi 1987: xi).

Recent battles over net neutrality worldwide expose the increasing consolidation of power of elite voices in driving the internet. This has brought into being what Parminder Singh (2010) terms "internet malls," or systems where preferential access is structured to make select powerful corporations more visible. While Singh discusses these issues mostly in relation to the disparity of resources to be offered in a pay-scale-run internet versus a free public internet, the implications go beyond the issue of resources to practices of how data is preserved, aggregated, and used. This is consistent with the perspective raised by Finn Brunton and Helen Nissenbaum (2013), who describe the need to prioritize and protect vulnerable non-control-holding internet users. They discuss the possibility of communally and locally developing data obfuscation tools and the potential that these tools hold to influence increasingly decentralized and autonomous internet use that escapes the dangers posed by surveillance regimes and sharing economies. At stake is a world where users have little to no power over the data they are consistently providing to "big data" repositories, which in turn can support both corporate and state power at the cost of citizen rights and freedoms.

Sharing Economy

In addition, we can also see how internet-centric communitarian language masks an economic system where the rich get richer. Today, far and wide, we hear the term "sharing economy" in relation to the internet. Yet what we hear less of is who actually benefits from that sharing. We see examples where any technology that monetizes user input is often treated as "sharing," with little critical scrutiny into how that technology functions or its associated political economies. While the term has circulated to frame internet economies as supportive of lateral or equal trade, consistent with early visions of the internet as supportive of a "gift economy," there is plenty of research that reveals macro-economic effects that generate economic inequality.

Indeed, critics argue that within many of the major sharing platforms today, such as AirBnB and Uber, the gifting appears to only go in one direction: from technology users to the owners of the platforms and those they serve. Decentralized uses of new technology were supposed to shape the world into a participatory culture (Jenkins et al. 2005), and we do at times see examples of this. But when another Silicon Valley company is purchased or makes an initial public offering on the stock exchange leading to the investment of billions of dollars in these companies, none of these funds are shared with the individual users whose "digital labor" built value for these companies (Fish & Srinivasan 2012). Several social media companies could thus be viewed as exploitative: aggregating labor without compensation, avoiding taxes through offshore accounts, avoiding unionization and the payment for laborer benefits, and migrating into new domains of industry (Fuchs 2015). And the result of this may shape disastrous macro-economic outcomes. For example, Instagram, with 13 employees, sold for $100 million in the same month within which Kodak, with tens of thousands of employees, went bankrupt (Ulanoff 2012).

If such is the pattern of the sharing economy, then where will the safeguards lie for fair, protected, and well-compensated working- and middle-class labor? These questions characterize the ethical and practical challenges that face media industries as they navigate the boundaries between creativity and capitalization, security and independence, and individualization and loose-knit "social" media collectivity (Deuze 2007). Digital labor may be the new "killer app" for these corporations, but do little to support social and economic justice.

Adam Fish (2015) discusses the double standards practiced by several internet corporations, accentuated as they spread the "opportunities" of providing access to the web across the globe through projects such as Facebook's internet-delivering drones. He claims that this establishes a pattern where technology-developing countries direct the internet's operation and growth, while offering it to others in substantially more commercialized and regulated forms. The internet is hardly open to these users, but instead constructed in the image of the access-providing corporation. Most troubling is the lack of intuitive ability to protest or undo the imbalance. We must ask: how does one protest against a Facebook internet-providing drone in the sky and out of our sight?

Fish notes that there is no process by which the elites that control technology can be easily stopped, and that indeed the current dynamic contributes to inequality in a number of arenas. For example, while a few musicians and video producers may use the internet to be discovered by millions, the vast majority of grassroots artists have been found to be even further distanced from the resources they need to sustain and succeed (Byrne 2013). A number of corporations that have productively used the scalability of the internet to create successful businesses have been purchased and incorporated into multinational and multiplatform media companies that in the process monopolize certain sectors of the internet (Patelis & Hatzopoulos 2013).

Such concerns around the privatized overtones of the internet relate to the early work of Saskia Sassen (1998) and later work by Karl Rethemeyer (2007) regarding the impact of such corporatization on the potential for decentralized and autonomous use of the internet. Sassen notes the changing architecture of the internet in influencing the emergence of "non-state-centered governance mechanisms" (1998: 545), which she argues have altered the meaning of territory, especially the transformation of the internet into "a contested space with considerable potential for segmentation and privatization. Perhaps the most important takeaway from her piece is the claim that "network power is not inherently distributive" (1998: 546).

Sassen points to the absence of excessive commercialization as the key factor in the internet's distributed nature, as we see even ostensibly participatory networks become increasingly more concentrated in power and resources. Rethemeyer (2007) discusses this increased concentration of commercialization and resources online in the context of government participation, concluding from a series of case studies that the internet is exacerbating the ongoing corporatization of state and federal government, silencing citizen voices and anti-hegemonic movements. The internet may be a decentralized network, but those who control the way information flows and is monetized are well equipped to exploit this architecture.

Neoliberalism in Action

Issues around technology and inequality shape not just poorer distant users of the global South but also the places and cultures where technology is produced. An example of such is the San Francisco Bay Area. This part of the world has long given birth to grassroots activist and social justice movements, from the anti-Vietnam war student protests to the Black Panther movement. It is also an important witness to the birth of the internet and the web, particularly via countercultural online communities dedicated to principles of environmentalism, economic equality, and the gift economy.

While various forms of activism focused on supporting the voiceless still exist within the Bay area region of Northern California, we note that the profitability of the internet industry can be tied to San Francisco's status as the most expensive city in the United States. It has become an increasingly visible flashpoint of gentrification in action, displacing immigrants, activists, and working-class laborers (Bort 2015). It is also a reminder that the effects of a supposedly ubiquitous infrastructure like the internet are *material*. The internet shapes and is shaped by people and places.

Critics point out that today's internet must be seen in relation to neoliberal policies and economics, which is increasingly seen as a desirable positive given the absence of more progressive or fundamentally democratic political choices: for example, the United States election between Hillary Clinton and Donald Trump or the "Brexit" issue regarding the United Kingdom leaving the European Union. Neoliberalism can be viewed as the outgrowth of increasingly close relationships forged between states and private corporations, as evidenced by increased deregulation (Martinez & Garcia 2000). As an intertwined set of economic and political systems, its effects have increasingly delegated public spaces and services to private corporations.

Our public spaces online are often managed and manipulated by for-profit corporations such as Facebook or Google, whose parent holding company is called Alphabet, Inc. Critics argue that such a neoliberal system supports the mirage of freedom while working to manipulate economic, political, and informational transactions. Yet we also know that "free" trade agreements such as NAFTA, a poster child of neoliberalism, have functioned to displace indigenous peoples, and galvanized the rise of indigenous-led social movements such as those of the Zapatistas of Mexico, who have fought against the privatization of their lands and lives (Cleaver 1998).

Within spaces of power and privilege in the United States, the collusion between major internet apostles and the US government is barely veiled, though largely left undiscussed by the popular media. Jared Cohen, a former State Department and current Google employee, has recently written a book with Eric Schmidt, chairman of Alphabet (and former CEO of Google), extolling the power of Western tools to "solve problems" (Cohen & Schmidt 2013), while failing to discuss that these tools are private and proprietary and that their use ultimately serves Google's bottom line. "Problems," from their perspective, represent a way of framing social or public conversations that are consensus-based or radically democratic. In another example, Megan Smith, a former manager at Google, became President Obama's Chief Technology Officer (Scola 2014). While many progressive activists decry the revolving door between Wall Street and the US government, few scrutinize a similar pattern in relation to Silicon Valley. Indeed, Silicon Valley is often treated as an unmitigated good, which is dangerous given its incredible economic and social power. The connections between technology corporations and the state must thus be unpacked rather than merely taken for granted.

Perilous Myths

This book cites ample scholarship that reveals that the internet as it stands is not the democracy-producing dream technology that it was perhaps imagined to be in its early days. We continue to live in a world where the internet continues to be portrayed as transcendent (Hayles 1999; Naude 2009), democratic, and transformative. But perhaps unlike some of our colleagues, we believe that in these imaginaries lie great value, and the potential for a rethinking of the internet in line with social, political, and economic justice. We must understand how transcendent ideas of the internet are socially or culturally constructed, and how they may be appropriated to support a democratic and just world "after the internet." Our six chapters reimagine technological networks in line with grassroots populations from the global North and South, and point to the potential of an internet that is *reassembled* alongside legal, environmental, and cultural factors to support these values.

Yet to truly take a step toward *situating* technology alongside these grassroots voices, we must do away with the mistaken presumption that the internet is largely autonomous from the many people, places, and infrastructures which go into its construction and, in turn, are shaped accordingly. Otherwise it becomes far too easy to give in to what psychotherapist Barry Richards has called *technophilia*, which "impedes rational discussion...and produce[s] referential or dismissive attitudes rather than realistic appraisal of social costs and benefits" (1993: 188).

In line with Richards' discussion, we can recognize that the internet, like any technology, should be viewed relative to the myths by which it has been described and evangelized. Myths are historical narratives that provide social meaning to individual lives and assist subjects in transcending the contradictions of their society (Lévi-Strauss 1978). They work to serve and support ideology – a discourse that concurrently seems to liberate and constrain social and cultural life (Moyers & Campbell 1988). They can be dystopic or utopic, yet may only loosely cohere with what one may learn from an engaged empirical analysis. As semiotician Roland Barthes so aptly stated: "Myth does not deny things; on the contrary, its function is to talk about them; simply, it purifies them, it makes them innocent, it gives them a natural and eternal justification, it gives them a clarity which is not that of an explanation but that of a statement of fact" (Barthes 2000: 143).

Technology critic Evgeny Morozov, who in his *To Save Everything, Click Here* (2013) consistently wrote "internet" in scare quotes, argued in an interview with CNN that "[t]he reason for putting 'the Internet' in quotes is simply to indicate that we have accumulated too many myths to continue without harming our own ability to arrive at wise policy"

(Leopold 2013). We agree with Morozov's points about myth and the "internet." We need to demystify the internet by viewing it as material and situated. This is one of the reasons we write this word with a lower case "i" throughout the book.

One of the most prominent myths of the internet is that it is universally undifferentiated, encompassing all knowledge regardless of place or culture. Yet we must recognize that a massive Chinese internet exists in parallel, rarely intersecting with the English-dominated platform that many take for granted (Qiang 2011), and that the information made visible by Western platforms such as Facebook or Google is algorithmically mediated, often resembling "echo chambers." We recognize that the internet can be spoken about along multiple categories: as an infrastructure (Musiani 2012), media network (Coleman 2010), or space for global communication (Hargittai 2007). Yet each of these is often described relative to myths that articulate the internet as a force to unite, expand, and connect people. It is assumed that "connection" is better, and that somehow with greater connectivity equality arises. Little is spoken about who owns these connections, who creates and manages the architectures of connectivity, and whose underlying epistemology drives the structure and network of connectivity. From this perspective, any singular framing of the internet is at best partial. And more damagingly, this universalizing myth dismisses the critical inquiry necessary to support grassroots democratic and activist objectives.

While myths can help individuals cope with the contradictions of modernity and point to a realm of the possible, the level of mythmaking and fetishization of the internet has reached a point where perhaps new myths need to be constructed. Richard Maxwell and Toby Miller ask us to counter the "myths that swirl around digital media convergence – managerial efficiency, experiential immediacy, global interactivity and interpersonal connectedness...with the histories of the environmental plunder and toxic sweatshops that have made old and new media possible" (2011: 595).

Myths about technologies both open and close realms of political possibility. Vincent Mosco says these qualities can "depoliticize speech but they can also open the door to a restoration of politics, to a deepening of political understanding"

(2004: 16). Thus myths, like metaphors, can communicate aspirations and intentions. They are persuasive stories we tell ourselves about our technologies and their near-mystical possibilities, obfuscations that gesture toward a potentiality.

Myths speak through metaphors that obscure the internet, situating it as something knowable by referencing familiar objects and practices. With respect to the internet, the metaphors are numerous and at times quite dated. The web may be an ocean we surf, a library we scan, an information super-highway we navigate, a market for e-commerce, or a community for friends and family. The web itself is a metaphor, invoking a complex structure that still maintains order. The internet is imagined as biological, forming a webbed media ecology. It is an agora, a public space for reasoned or passionate debate. We upload to the cloud. Oceans, libraries, clouds, webs, markets, ecologies, democracies, highways – these are all metaphors for the internet. Words are thus often used as symbolic replacements for the phenomenological world itself. In this way, metaphors are unavoidable and each has its moment. But metaphors like myths are not empty signifiers. Instead, they frame the internet in ways that are socially and politically enacted – influencing the very means by which it is understood, used, and regulated. Metaphors are thus often incorporated into larger and more inclusive systems of belief, or mythologies.

Mosco (2004) and James Curran (2012) have identified and deconstructed numerous myths in relation to the internet. They reveal how the internet has been mythologized as capable of bringing about an end of history with the arrival of a capitalist democracy fueled by an information economy. The role of the state as a monopoly of coercive political power would diminish as vigilant citizen journalists arose and gate-keepers disappeared. Another myth sees environmentally harmful practices of mining, processing, and shipping atom-based goods replaced by the production of weightless bit-based information. Yet another is the myth that the internet would bring about world peace because, naturally, oppositional groups would take to the internet and, without the intimidation of meeting face-to-face, overcome their differences through generative discourses. And finally, another posits that the internet, reducing the advantages associated with economies of scale, would place small businesses and massive corporations on a level playing field (for these myths of the internet, see Curran 2012). These are but a few of the myths of the internet that have captured the popular imaginary in ways that support the practices and aspirations of those with the persuasive power of public myth-making.

Myths have consequences. For instance, the myth of the end of history, advanced most notably by Francis Fukuyama (1992), fails to consider how democracy and capitalism, and their linkages, are in a constant state of flux and negotiation within which the internet plays an important though not decisive role (Curran 2012). To claim that the internet automatically results in direct democracy and a kinder, gentler capitalism is to ignore the role played by more traditional, grassroots politics. Similarly, the myth of direct digital democracy is challenged by the fact that only 14 percent of Americans have produced a simple blog (Curran 2012), with numbers far smaller in other nations worldwide. Faith in this myth of digital participation and democracy places undue attention on technology and away from structural and institutional inequalities in political voice and literacy (Couldry 2010).

When we think of myth and the history of the internet, it is hard not to consider former US Vice President Al Gore. In 1991, Gore wrote that "high-speed networks must be built that tie together millions of computers, providing capabilities that we cannot even imagine" (1991: 150). In 1994, Gore gave a speech in Los Angeles stating: "Our current information industries – cable, local telephone, long distance telephone, television, film, computers, and others – seem headed for a Big Crunch/Big Bang of their own" (Gore 1994). A few months later, in Buenos Aires, he discussed the potential of this Big Crunch to create "networks of distributed intelligence" that would "spread participatory democracy" (quoted in Brooks & Boal 1995: xii). Thus, Gore developed a myth about internet democratization which he then advocated for throughout the world.

Then on March 9, 1999, Gore told CNN's Wolf Blitzer, "During my service in the United States Congress, I took the initiative in creating the internet." Gore's remarks were made at a historical point when "the fascination with markets, privatization and deregulation and a correlate antipathy to government regulation – seemed to be on the wane" (Streeter 2003: 655). The internet would be the new myth that would fuel financial investment, creative work, political vision, and citizens' involvement. With Yahoo, Amazon, and eBay's Initial Public Offerings (IPOs) in 1996, 1997, and 1998, the myth seemed to become a self-fulfilling prophecy. On the campaign trail, Gore attempted to link himself to the powers of this new communication platform (Fish 2017b).

Politicians who have made the internet central to their campaigns are notable for the myths they concoct. Consider the case in which Vermont Governor Howard Dean and his campaign director Joe Trippi borrowed language from the free and open source software movement (FOSS) during the 2004 Democratic Party primaries, discussing theirs as an "open source campaign" (Kreiss 2011). This argument can be tied to the rhetoric of Silicon Valley and the rising excitement of participatory culture. Making these connections enabled journalists to write about the campaign through powerful symbols (Kreiss 2011: 373).

The presidential campaigns of Dean, Barack Obama, and recently Donald Trump are notable for their creative use of the internet for organizing. Obama, like Dean and Gore, used the internet as a myth on the campaign trail. In a speech on July 13, 2012, Obama argued, "The internet didn't get invented on its own. Government research created the internet so that companies could make money off the internet." This remark, unscrupulously edited, started a debate about who "made" the internet. The *Wall Street Journal* accused Obama of being wrong, stating that it was a corporation, Xerox PARC, and not the government that should be given credit (Crovitz 2012). *Slate* disagreed, stating that the President was correct, as the government funded what became the internet (Manjoo 2012). *Time*'s opinion was that it was neither the state nor corporations that invented the internet, but genius individuals like the creator of HTML, Tim Berners-Lee (McCracken 2012). Finally, the *New York Times* disagreed with all of the above, crediting the creation of the internet to the people, pointing to the community of open source developers (Johnson 2012). Thus these conflicting accounts of internet history reveal a political jockeying over whose myths hold power, and therefore shape technical, economic, and political practices around how the internet may continue to take form (Fish 2017b).

There are also dystopic myths that we can associate with the internet. Toby Miller, a scholar who focuses his recent work on environmentalism and technology, wrote in a 2016 Facebook posting:

> A deregulated, individuated, technologized world makes consumers into producers, frees the disabled from confinement, encourages new subjectivities, rewards intellect and competitiveness, links people across cultures, and allows billions of flowers to bloom in a post-political cornucopia. It is a bizarre utopia. People fish, film, fornicate, and finance from morning to midnight. Consumption is privileged, production is discounted, and labor is forgotten.

Miller's position resonates with some of the criticisms that we raised in the previous section. Yet his point also speaks to that which seems to be tantalizing about the moment in which we live today: the sense of freedom, liberty, and decentralization that empowers internet subjectivity. He explains that this false sense comes at the cost of many traditional values associated with community, governance and the public sphere, cultural traditions, and more.

As we discuss next, our intention in this book is to use myth productively while recognizing that, in and of themselves, unifying dystopic or utopic myths do little to help us understand or imagine the internet in relation to the complex social, political, cultural, and economic practices that must always be viewed alongside technology. We thus argue throughout this book that the internet is better understood as an *assemblage* of heterogeneous people, devices, contexts, and meanings. In this sense, our concern is neither with the existence of myth nor with its undeniable value, but with the question of who makes such myths and how much power they hold in shaping the agendas of some at the cost of others.

Fragments and Assemblages

Artist and critic Zach Blas has written persuasively about the dangers of the "post" language that seems to describe so many phenomena today. He argues that we no longer pay attention to the term that follows "post" and instead embrace a sort of existential nihilism, a "haziness...a blanket generalization that is an empty descriptor" (Blas 2014: 85).

Blas goes on to apply this critique to the internet, arguing that instead of thinking "post" internet, we must think "contra" internet, where internet practices can be identified that overturn the hegemony enacted by the political and corporate forces we have discussed. Contra-internet aesthetics opens up a space for possibility, and builds upon important critiques of the internet, from standardization and quantification, to rampant privatization (Blas 2014). Blas describes a number of aesthetic and political projects that work with network technology to expose the fallacies of existing systems to shape better alternatives, such as public stagings of drone crashes, mesh network efforts to support transgender activism, darknet networks for Occupy activists, and mobile phone GPS systems to aid migrants crossing the US–Mexico border. Each of these, he explains, contains the "aesthetic potentiality to make the political alternative" (Blas 2014).

It is in this spirit that this book's chapters reimagine the internet through four perspectives, split evenly across the global North and South. At all these sites, we see how what the internet is and stands for can shift away from its increasingly centralized, commodified, and "personalized" hegemonic incarnation to something more in line with the original spirit of it as a network technology to support grassroots communication. We explore this rethinking of the internet in relation to indigenous communities worldwide, hacker activists dedicated to free speech and transparency, revolutionaries of the Arab Spring, and policymakers and social entrepreneurs fighting for data protection and privacy in Iceland.

What brings these chapters together is their treatment of the internet as an assemblage, a collection of heterogeneous actors, places, and objects. Not only are the technologies that comprise the internet assemblages, but the cases we share are also examples of assemblage, owing to the ways in which they rethink technology alongside a number of environmental, institutional, and legal factors.

Gilles Deleuze and Félix Guattari (1987) describe an assemblage as a set of complex systems constituted by the convergence of bodies, ideas, technologies, and other transecting entities. Deleuze stated: "In assemblages you find states of things, bodies, various combinations of bodies, hodgepodges; but you also find utterances, modes of expression, and whole regimes of signs" (2007: 176–7).

To recast our understandings of what an assembled internet is, we must do away with what Deleuze describes as an arborescent treatment of matter and knowledge as hierarchical, tree-like, fixed, or entity-centric. In contrast with a static understanding of that which is, Deleuze and Guattari introduce the metaphor of the "rhizome," an underground stem that is dynamic, multiplicitous, decentralized. They explain that the rhizome "has no beginning or end; it is always in the middle, between things, interbeing, intermezzo…. The planar movement of the rhizome resists chronology and organization, instead favoring a nomadic system of growth and propagation" (Deleuze & Guattari 1987: 32–3).

To treat the internet rhizomatically must involve doing away with stable, singular, and hierarchical thinking (or myths) of it. This is not merely a philosophical shift but indeed in-line with the way RAND engineer Paul Baran, the inventor of the packet-switching technology that facilitates data sharing, has described the internet. Baran's description highlights the "heterogeneous within the ephemeral" and the instability of networked communications "infused with movement and change" (Marcus & Saka 2006: 102). One, therefore, must thus see the design and development of technology as a type of non-linear layering:

> The process of technological development is like building a cathedral…. Over the course of several hundred years new people come along and each lays down a block on top of the old foundations, each saying, "I built a cathedral." … If you are not careful, you can con yourself into believing that you did the most important part. (Paul Baran, cited in Hafner & Lyon 1996: 79–80)

The internet is an assemblage of hardware, software, corporations, government regulations, code, practices, users, and engineers in a constant state of flux and emergence. A subset of scholarship in science and technology studies (STS) employed a similar approach in its *sociotechnical analysis*, focusing on the interplay between institutions and technical infrastructure of the internet as a way to explore emerging patterns of use and governance (DeNardis 2012; Musiani 2012). Though this work often does not explicitly employ the use of the term "assemblage," its perspective toward analyzing and discussing the intersections of technology and society speaks to an assemblage-like understanding. The work of the STS scholars we cite throughout the book reveals the value in moving beyond a static or unidirectional view of technology and its "effects" toward instead seeing technology users, institutions, infrastructure, policies, computational attributes, and more, as co-constituted.

After the Internet

The assemblages we share in this book's following five chapters represent a reflection on a world "after the internet." This book's title is a play on Terry Eagleton's *After Theory*, which criticizes the limitations of postmodern cultural theory. According to Eagleton, postmodernism is ill equipped to deal with material political problems because it "rejects totalities, universal values, grand historical narratives, solid foundations to human existence and the possibility of objective knowledge" (2003: 13). Postmodernism may give way to the nihilistic relativism that Blas critiques in his writings on contra-internet aesthetics. What is needed, according to Eagleton, is critical inquiry into the means for social solidarity – that which brings us together. *After Theory* implores scholars not to focus on either the grand nor the minute, but to argue about the "real life" issues of morality, revolution, and the problems associated with fundamentalism.

We take this politically aware and middle-range approach to the study of the internet. In titling our book *After the Internet*, we align ourselves with Eagleton's approach to consider the mechanisms by which internet technologies are developed and deployed to support economic, cultural, social, and political justice, not as articulated from afar but as emergent from the communities across the world who serve as this book's protagonists. Our use of this title is both playful and tactical. The theoretical and applied scholarship we share is of our world rather than some imagined future "after the internet." Yet by using the word "after" in our title, we wish to provoke an imagination that is respectful of contemporary practices. The world our cases describe and imagine is not a world where the internet fails to exist, but is instead shaken from its current incarnation.

We take issue with approaches to internet culture that too emphatically celebrate what is unique about a world fragmented by seemingly infinite possibilities for identity politics. Today, many articles are published in media studies that focus on the curious rituals of small online communities and their semiotic or performative modalities. We are responsible for some of this relativistic scholarship ourselves (Khalikova & Fish 2016; Srinivasan 2017), which is conducted with the intention of *provincializing* our understandings, or seeing them with the matrices of culture, context, and politics. Yet we cannot hone in on the local without thinking about how these examples may travel or intervene in the very bases by which networks, technologies, or infrastructures are deployed or constructed. Our chapters attempt to bring together the microscopic and the macroscopic, seeing the mesoscopic interplay between scalable theories and specific contexts and vernaculars.

After the Internet is an attempt to conceptualize internet theory after decades of overwhelming and at times silencing myths of the internet. While each of our chapters discusses a unique subcultural fluorescence, together they also illustrate how various local and "global" publics interact and shape one other. Indeed, it is true that there are ample examples of how localized political powers develop from the temporary autonomous zones that may be supported by digital media tools and environments. But we are also interested in how these seemingly local events may impact the formation of larger-scale systems and networks, and perhaps the internet itself. As Ramesh Srinivasan has argued (2014), it may be more interesting to consider what Tahrir Square can teach us about the internet rather than vice versa. What an internet "after the internet" may look like can be imagined when one learns from local assemblages such as those we share across this book's four case studies.

The examples presented in the following chapters describe processes by which technological components are placed within an assemblage of other elements to shape the aspirations of indigenous communities across the world, hacktivists, Arab Spring revolutionaries, and entrepreneurs and bureaucrats fighting for data protection. Each case reveals how elements of the internet are *disassembled* and give rise to new forms of *reassembly*. The chapters together reveal how the internet can no longer be seen as inseparable from the places, people, laws, and infrastructures of our world. It no longer serves economic, political, social, or environmental justice to continue to treat the internet as autonomous, detached, or neutral.

Chapter 1 reveals the power of fusing culture with technology in how we think about grassroots assemblages around the internet that involve culturally diverse communities worldwide, with an eye in particular toward indigenous peoples. It presents three cases whereby diverse global and indigenous communities have reimagined network technology infrastructures, such as the internet and mobile telephony. The assemblages it describes situate the internet alongside the cosmologies of these communities, "collective" economic models they have that are in direct contrast with increasingly monopolistic telecommunications companies and neoliberal internet corporations, and the environmental topographies of local places. The internet in this chapter is recast as an assemblage that brings together network technology with *beliefs, values, economics*, and *environments*.

Our second chapter discusses the extra-judicial criminalization and persecution of hacktivists, activists dedicated to exposing information around corporate and governmental abuse. We describe the work of hacktivists to create and exploit liminal zones of the internet. Our point in this chapter is that to best understand these dynamics one must see the internet not as stabilized or autonomous but instead as layered by a number of policing practices, which place networked technology in a precarious relationship with several legal, policing, and technological practices. This chapter's contribution therefore is to illuminate assemblages that are at the center of the battle for the internet and the values for which it stands. This assemblage includes legal statutes, technologies that aid and disrupt surveillance, and three extra-judicial policing practices employed by states and hacktivists: *selfie-incrimination, versioning*, and *edgework*. It is a reminder that despite myths of being friction-free, internet technologies and the meanings for which they stand are refracted through the prisms of national boundaries, histories, and institutions.

With an eye primarily toward the Arab Spring, our third chapter considers the wave of grassroots movements and revolutions that our world has witnessed since late 2010. This chapter exposes a troubling myth that sees the internet as interchangeable with terms such as "Facebook revolution." The assemblages it describes view the internet in relation with other modes of building and mobilizing networks, such as labor movements, mosques, or neighbourhood councils. Describing the case of Egypt and Tahrir Square in detail, this chapter argues that we must see the internet and digital networks as part of an assemblage that brings together *offline networks and spaces*, *"older" media* such as television and radio, *economic and political institutions*, and *physical bodies* in shaping political activism.

Our fourth and final chapter considers the troubles with personal data, increasingly routed to massive privatized data centers, made accessible for surveillance along the way. We consider how privacy-minded individuals, activists, and corporations are attempting to make Iceland into a data haven. In this way, Icelandic data activists and politicians have assembled an alternative imaginary of "the cloud," one that may represent fertile ground for experiments in technology-assisted democracy. The assemblages this chapter describes frame the internet in relation to policies and laws of a liberal Northern Atlantic nation-state and the increasingly global concern around unchecked surveillance. This chapter speaks to the realization by technology users across the world that their uses of the internet are no longer anonymous but instead subject to capture, surveillance, and tracking. It further speculates on what this means for public actions and speech, or whether we have entered a digital world where the public sphere has become increasingly threatened. As we move forward with supporting the privacy of users, we must think about what type of public spaces we can still support in our world, and how speech and expression in such environments can be protected. The internet in this chapter is thus recast as an assemblage that includes *national policy, extra-legal attempts to capture and manipulate data,* and a *cultural vision of social liberalism* that holds ties to classical post-Enlightenment philosophy.

From our perspective, the practices described in each of our four chapters are complementary in that they intentionally contest the forces that dominate how the internet and new technologies are evangelized, designed, and deployed. They interrupt our current moment of *technodeterminism*, where we all too easily assume that the technologies around us are here to stay and to be passively used as prescribed.

These cases should not be blindly embraced but understood as responses to a world where the internet has increasingly come to benefit the agendas of elites at the cost of others. By opening up the conversation around "who" it is that creates, designs, deploys, assembles, and reassembles technology, the previously peripheral has the opportunity to become central, the fragments can become modes for reassembly, and networks and technologies can be rethought of in the image of activist causes. Our aim in the following chapters will be to inspire critical thinking of what a world "after the internet" may look like for grassroots communities and activists across the world – one that blends their local concerns and creativity with the need to achieve scalable change and transformation.

1
Reimagining Technology with Global Communities

In the summer of 2009, Ramesh Srinivasan, one of this book's authors, was able to arrange a trip to the Sepik River of Papua New Guinea (PNG) thanks to a local guide, Seby Mai, whom he met in the nearby town of Wewak. The Sepik is famous for its dramatic landscapes featuring winding rivers and swamps with villages interspersed every few miles. The village communities of this region are known to have maintained relatively distinct indigenous practices of worship, performance, and language. While Pidgin and English were "taught" to the local people by the colonial missionaries, PNG's several hundred indigenous languages continue to thrive.

In line with the story we share, we recognize how important it is to be wary of the ethical transgressions, historical and contemporary, and heed the words of scholars who are wary of social science work that has contributed to the objectification of tribal and non-Western peoples worldwide (Clifford 1989; Hayes & Hayes 1970). An experience of other places or peoples may perhaps be better understood as one of the "borderland" (Badone 2004; Rosaldo, Calderón, & Salvadívar 1991), a theory that recognizes the heterogeneity of any place, culture, or community. Our telling of this story is thus not intended to essentialize the "other" but instead to reveal the potential agency and ingenuity of all peoples.

Having reached the river long after dusk following several hours of transportation via cars, buses, and donkey carts,

Srinivasan and Seby were picked up by the guide's brother in his large dugout canoe. Seby explained that night-time was a time of great success for his community's crocodile hunting trade. He and his family would try to capture these reptiles alive and then imprison, feed, and skin them. Yet to find them in the river, the hunter would have to detect their luminescent eyes in the pitch dark. The days of flashlights had long passed, however, because batteries were too expensive and in short supply. And there was no working electricity in any of the villages except for those communities that had been able to purchase generators.

How, then, could such hunting occur in the dark? To answer, Seby's brother pulled a mobile phone out of his pocket along with a mirror and used these together to project a light in different directions, illuminating the night-time sky.

This anecdote is notable because it reveals how the tool of the mobile phone was repurposed to support local economic and cultural practices. The phone was not used to make or receive calls, let alone to browse the internet or send text messages. But it was appropriated in an unanticipated, creative manner. It is a reminder of Tim Ingold's expression that we "know as we go" (2000: 229). Ingold's point is that knowledge is revealed through actions, practices, and movements. The creative repurposing of the mobile phone, rather than the tool itself, is an example of knowledge in action.

We introduced this chapter with this experience within PNG to emphasize the power of *agency* that exists within communities across the world, and particularly those of the global South, that have recently been exposed to the internet and new digital technologies. This is a reminder that despite centuries of colonialism, indigenous and non-Western peoples are neither permanently marginalized, nor inherently dependent on institutions or infrastructures produced by first-world elites. Nor are they merely objectified users of new technology. Indeed, despite systematic marginalization, as various global communities engage with new technologies they practice what Steven Jackson (2014) describes as "innovation within constraint." This is in direct contrast to the myth that sees internet users worldwide as passive beneficiaries of existing systems and infrastructures, waiting for first-world hand-me-downs.

This chapter presents three cases to reveal how indigenous communities have reimagined network technologies in line with their visions, aspirations, and practices. Like our story from PNG, the examples we share are of assemblages crafted by diverse communities across the world. These assemblages reveal that the internet and new media technology cannot be separated from the *belief systems*, *knowledges*, and *local geographies*, *politics*, and *economics* of community life. Instead, they are interconnected as assemblages.

In the sections that follow, we discuss much of the literature around the internet that objectifies indigenous and marginalized global communities, and specifically the misguided notion of the "digital divide." We discuss how theories of "information access" and their implementation threaten rather than support cultural diversity. In contrast, we argue that we must learn from diverse communities as we rethink epistemologies around technology use that are mistakenly embraced as universal truth. We can instead gain a great deal by learning from assemblages that fuse cultural practices and beliefs with technology.

Digital Divides and Their Apostles

This book's introduction described the danger in treating the internet as autonomous, sovereign, and immune from critique. When we treat technology as such, it becomes a "stable reference" rather than a point of inquiry. This is consistent with Martin Heidegger's (1954) concept of *Gestell*, which refers to the means by which technology "enframes" – or presents an all-encompassing view of – what human existence is or should be. Such a treatment of technology evangelizes it in some platonic and immaterial form while failing to imagine or reflect upon what else may be (Ciborra 2002).

Treating the internet and new technologies as fixed and magical gives rise to the problematic "digital divide" mission of blindly connecting the many billions to the internet. Part of what fuels the myth of the digital divide is the notion that a single internet can or does exist, and that extending access to networked technologies (including mobile phones) is all that is needed to bring about some ambiguously defined form of development or empowerment. Yet as Nicole Zillien and Eszter Hargittai (2009) point out, "the Internet cannot be assumed to be 'inherently good or inherently bad.'...Like all other technologies, the affordances of the internet are related to its history, its design, and the context of its adoption and usage" (2009: 274). These scholars' research on different forms of technological use across social strata demonstrates the absence of a single internet, instead emphasizing the variety of starting points, literacies, belief systems, and points of contingency that shape the lives of users across the world.

A quintessential example of the universalizing approach taken around the digital divide can be seen via the actions of Google, the world's most profitable company. At the TED 2014 conference, Google co-founder Larry Page explained how his company was dedicated to bringing "hope" to peoples across the world, while citing an advertisement of a Kenyan farmer thanking the company for providing his community with useful information (Page 2014). Moments before, Page had spoken with great pride about the Google Loon project, which deploys balloons over the stratosphere to spread internet access to "dark spots" in the world.

Both these examples reveal Page's presumption that access to the Google version of the internet is merely a technical challenge to be bridged rather than part of a complex assemblage that brings together technologies with a number of cultural, social, and ethical dynamics. Google, blindly assumed to be an unambiguous good, will spread access to "its" internet. It is dangerously assumed that poorer and non-Western communities "wish" for internet access on Google's terms, even if this internet is tiered, meaning skewed toward advertisers who have paid Google to be made visible.

Similar to Google's efforts, in 2014 Mark Zuckerberg, CEO of Facebook, announced his company's "Connectivity Lab," which will deploy drone technologies to spread internet access worldwide (Zuckerberg 2014). For Zuckerberg, as for Page, "connecting" everyone to his company's version of the internet is merely a technical challenge. Yet both of these examples fail to question what such connectivity looks like, who would drive it, and what obstacles it faces. If a user community, for example in rural Africa, prefers an alternative, non-commercial, and relatively more open version of the internet, how can it protest against an automated system in the sky?

As Lisa Parks and Nicole Starosielski (2015) argue, technical statements of internet access pose as neutral while masking a number of hidden agendas. Like any technology, the infrastructures by which internet access is provided must be read relative to the social, political, or economic arrangements by which they were designed and deployed. Google Loon or Facebook Free Basics, supported by the Connectivity Lab, must be seen as assemblages in their own right, and dissected to unpack the values and political economies with which they are associated. Yet these arrangements are mostly impossible to decipher when the balloons or drones we speak of are high up in the sky and far out of range of our proverbial "sight" (Fish 2015). The issue is echoed when we speak of the underwater fiber-optic cables that form the physical infrastructure of the internet. These may seem neutral and equalizing, yet they actually work to reinforce unequal geographies, as demonstrated, for example, by the few connections linking the formerly colonized continents of the global South (South America and Africa).

An analytical look at the global internet as it stands reveals geographies of inequality consistent with the asymmetric flows of people, capital, images, and media that are part of our world today. In a powerful narration of neoliberal globalization, anthropologist Arjun Appadurai (1990) described these phenomena in his article titled "Difference and Disjuncture in the Global Cultural Economy." Appadurai's theories are supported by research around the theme of "digital inequality," whose findings argue that the benefits provided by internet use tend to be disproportionately enjoyed by those already in positions of privilege as opposed to their poorer counterparts (Zillien & Hargittai 2009). Such work connects and exposes the neoliberal social and political climates that affect what the internet means and how it is interwoven with everyday life. Similarly, in her work examining the intersection of social and digital inequality in natural disasters, Mirca Madianou (2015) finds similar consistencies between social inequalities and the asymmetric means by which digital resources are wielded to support user communities.

A number of scholars have thus shown that access to the internet on average reinforces rather than resolves social and economic inequality (Castells 2000; DiMaggio, Hargittai, Celeste, & Shafer, 2004; Hargittai 2008; Zillien & Hargittai 2009). Unsurprisingly, those with higher economic, political, and social status tend to have better technical equipment, faster connections, and stronger digital literacy (Hargittai 2008; Howard, Busch, & Sheets 2010; Warschauer 2004), defined as the skills needed to use a digital resource in an autonomous, individualized, and effective way.

The myth that spreading technologies empowers all equally is further rebutted by scholarship that reveals how digital technologies disproportionately empower specific geographies and peoples at the cost of others (Sassen 2002). The majority of the world's population tends to be left absent from determining how technologies could or should diffuse. The term "silent majority" in this case can be safely replaced with "silent billions." Even ethnographic research of technology use often pushes commercial and consumerist agendas, opaquely implying that there is a "win-win" in the spread of technology. This includes the studies of former Nokia researcher Jan Chipchase (2007), who has identified community-specific activities associated with people's uses of mobile phones worldwide, yet somehow presumed that this is evidence of everyone wishing to be part of a "global conversation."

The pernicious impacts of an unscrutinized global technology market are apparent when examining the ecological and environmental effects wrought by the diffusion of digital systems and tools. These devastating effects disproportionately affect and traumatize communities on the margins of economic and political power, particularly those in the developing world. Richard Maxwell and Toby Miller (2012) discuss the negative implications of the rise of technocapitalism from this perspective. Through a series of related case studies, they describe the international supply chain of Apple, Las Maquiladoras electronic workers of Mexico, and the "ragpickers" of toxic sludge in the global South as examples of the varied environmental repercussions facing different laborers and poorer communities as a result of massive expansion in the production, distribution, and use of digital technologies.

The authors describe the habitual consumption and discarding of TVs, computer monitors, cell phones, and other electronic devices within these examples as e-waste. Maxwell and Miller argue that the global supply chain perpetuates harmful electronic production practices, and call for the media, policymakers, and activists to play a larger role in exposing the devastating ecological consequences brought about by the "digital revolution" to communities worldwide.

Yet in contrast to these findings, the mainstream media tend to feed a naïve narrative that equates internet access with emancipation (Bellware 2016; Chhabra 2016; Goel 2015). For example, while we hear today about how the spread of technology has influenced the growth of a technology-fluent middle class in specific cities in India, Nigeria, or the Philippines (Haseloff 2005), what we may not consider is how these forms of economic mobility may reinforce larger patterns of inequality, whether through harming the environment, spurring on unsustainable urbanization, or displacing these digital laborers from their cultural heritage and identity. In this regard, cultural studies scholar Raka Shome has pointed out how call centers, despite their democratizing hype, in fact erase identity, body, language, and agency. Work along these lines has also pointed to the means by which these centers have shifted sleep cycles (Shome 2006) and unhinged cultural and social traditions, leaving these center laborers largely powerless and voiceless.

In a *New York Times* piece entitled "The Banality of 'Don't Be Evil,'" WikiLeaks publisher Julian Assange takes aim at "digital divide" efforts spearheaded by partnerships between technology corporations and Western governments. Assange explains that the supposedly democratizing missions of spreading technology are in fact intended to bring about a world where "[c]ommodities just become more marvellous; young, urban professionals sleep, work and shop with greater ease and comfort; democracy is insidiously subverted by technologies of surveillance, control is enthusiastically rebranded as 'participation'; and our present world order of systematized domination, intimidation and oppression continues, unmentioned, un-afflicted or only faintly perturbed" (Assange 2013).

Such is a world, according to Assange, where elites and Western corporations drive a discussion of internet progress and futures while continuing to objectify users across the world. Adam Fish (2015) echoes these concerns, arguing that a narrowly controlled and commercialized internet is passed on by elites in the Western world to others in positions of less privilege. Fish stresses the consolidation of power among growing technology companies and governments to dictate the future of the internet. In contrast to this, by learning from grassroots community assemblages that fuse cultural practices with technology, we can shift whom we listen to. In so doing, we can imagine alternative destinies for technology in our world to better support agendas of social and economic justice.

Thinking Locally

The internet must thus be seen not as an autonomous "cloud," but instead as interwoven with social, political, and technical systems and structures (Fuchs 2007). Assemblage theory, described in this book's introduction, opens up our thinking about elements both internal to the technology (such as its technical elements and codes of software and hardware) and external to it, bringing into play elements from our PNG story such as the crocodile hunters, their boats, the time of day, and their belief systems and practices.

Faye Ginsburg (2008), a visual and media anthropologist who for many years has studied how media technologies can be repurposed to support indigenous voices and agendas, has argued that we must dispense with the exceptionalist ways in which we speak about the digital divide to instead learn from "strategic traditionalism," or projects that are ethical, collaborative, and praxis-based and respectful of diverse cultural protocols that shape the flow and control of knowledge within communities. These efforts would learn from the literacy practices of local communities. We note that literacy can be best understood as a local, cultural, and collective practice of encoding, decoding, expressing, and reflecting; influencing the "skills and understandings involved in using [technologies] to locate, evaluate, and use information" (Warschauer 2004: 13).

Ginsburg (2008) discusses three efforts that embody her concept of strategic traditionalism: an Inuit television network started in the remote Arctic outpost of Nunavut; a for-profit Aboriginal youth media storytelling website; and an animation network called Raven Tales. Across all three, a few common themes emerge: the project's "center" is community-based, the project and any revenue it gathers are owned by community members, and the voices that drive the project's implementation and content are created, curated, and produced by community members. These efforts are complex assemblages that consider technologies in tandem with a number of other local institutions, people, and environmental factors. For example, the Nunavut project cannot be understood simply as a television station but as an assemblage that incorporates the many infrastructures needed to establish such a station, including electricity, equipment, network bandwidth, and regulatory agreements. Ginsburg describes how this effort gave birth to a number of Inuit "media labs," nomadic technology centers for youth across Inuit territory that could shape their participation in the incipient network. What these media labs stand for is determined by the Inuit, rather than an internet-providing drone in the sky and its parent company thousands of miles away.

What we see in these examples is a defiance of homogenizing principles such as "information wants to be free." Scholars including Jane Anderson (2009) and Haidy Geismar (2005) have done pioneering work with indigenous communities to re-envision software languages, databases, infrastructures, and interfaces as grassroots community assemblages. Geismar has examined indigenous Vanuatu concepts of "relationality" and attempted to implement these in a digital museum system operated by community leaders. Anderson is a leading scholar exploring indigenous notions of intellectual property. We also note the work of Robin Boast, who has long been interested in rethinking classification and object description in museums and cultural heritage institutions.

Bringing a number of these ideas together, ethnic studies scholar Kim Christen and colleagues (Bell, Christen, & Turin 2013) have reconsidered digital museum and archival portals from the perspective of indigenous communities with whom they collaborate. Christen (2012) notes in her collaborations with the Warrumungu tribe of Central Australia how discussions of cultural issues respected the different roles of members within the community. She argues that one can think of technology similarly, and has thus developed the Mukurtu open source platform, which allows digital objects to be shared in accord with community-based protocols of access that respect kinship, age, gender, and more. The digital platform is reconfigured within these projects to mirror ever-evolving cultural practices and community-based values.

Working with assemblage theory, one can reimagine technology from the perspectives of local cultures and communities. User communities can take apart the tools, networks, systems, and infrastructures that have entered their world and recombine these into technologies that more meaningfully serve their purposes. And these elements need not be solely digital technologies but can also include other materials, bodies, or environmental elements.

Scholars, activists, and the larger public can learn from how diverse user communities worldwide *provincialize* technology, appropriating or adopting a tool or system within an environment far removed from its Western, "modern" origins. E. Gabriella Coleman (2010) has argued that this intellectual turn shifts our understanding of technology in three ways: (1) whom it represents and in what manners; (2) what theories, motifs, or vernaculars best describe technology's global migration; and (3) the emergent prosaics of technology, including how it reinforces and/or unhinges existing themes of human life.

One emerging vernacular considers the *recycling of modernity*, in the words of Ravi Sundaram (2009), and relatedly the *repair cultures* that have emerged around the asymmetric diffusion of digital tools and e-waste. Steven Jackson (2014) has described repair cultures where truths of erosion, breakdown, and decay overwhelm Western myths of innovation. His work has centered on the breakdown of the modern infrastructural ideal (Graham & Marvin 2001) and the creative, resilient practices of communities to repair the tools that were dumped in landfills and left to die under the terms of their planned obsolescence. It is important to respect and understand these practices of repair as they, alongside a range of other informal economy practices, speak to a world where survival within harsh environmental and economic constraints is precarious yet paramount.

These recycling and repair practices are at odds with trite statements of how the expansion of technology makes us all connected or global citizens, implying an equality which does not exist. Instead, these are examples of "globalization from below" (Della Porta, Andretta, Mosca, & Reiter 2006), defying Western scripts of usability, digital citizenship, and digital divides. It is high time to move past seeing digital tools as vehicles of Western modernity (Sennett 2008), which "presume the logic of a God's eye view and an agentic designer" (Philip, Irani, & Dourish 2010: 6).

We discuss three collaborations in the remainder of this chapter where the internet and new technologies are placed into assemblages with the values, practices and knowledges of indigenous communities in Southern California, rural New Mexico, and Oaxaca, Mexico. The first two cases involve collaborative design work with Native communities while the Oaxacan case reflects recent ethnographic fieldwork.

Indigenous Digital Networks: Tribal Peace

Our first case, Tribal Peace, is a multi-year collaboration with 19 Kumeyaay and Luiseno Native American reservations located in arid regions within San Diego County in Southern California. These communities, owing to a history of violence and persecution, had been moved onto reservations as long as a century ago, displacing them from traditional forms of subsistence, such as horticulture and fishing. The dispersion of these reservations fragmented the connections between tribal members, resulting in a deep cultural loss of heritage and identity, as seen in the erosion of language, traditions, and indigenous medicines.

A digital environment, Tribal Peace, was designed to leverage a technology infrastructure of wireless towers for these communities funded by governmental and commercial subsidies. This infrastructure, the "Tribal Digital Village," had to navigate a physically harsh topography and landscape, winds of over 100 mph, intense amounts of dust and dirt, steep mountains, searing heat, dazzling sunlight, and the ever-present risk of earthquakes and landslides. Its success would require

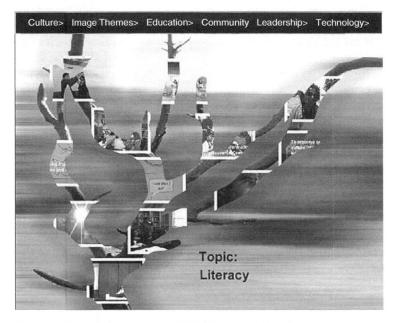

Figure 1.1   Interface of the Tribal Peace Native American system

learning from the communities living on this land. As sociologist Christian Sandvig describes:

> While one might think of the corporate engineers that developed and sold these towers, antennas, and radios as the experts on them, in fact the user of a device who is intimately familiar with its operation in their local context often has far more information about its performance characteristics and uses...their approach provided some innovative engineering. (Sandvig 2013: 188)

It is rare for urban scientists and engineers to think of infrastructure as local or place-specific. Indeed, like top-down myths of the internet, internet and other technology infrastructures are often seen as "black boxes" (Mansell 1990) – manufactured within laboratories to be exported far and wide. Yet developing and deploying a technology infrastructure is also an example of a local assemblage, in this case fusing technical components from the San Diego Supercomputer Center with mountaintops, soil, local carpentry, and metalwork, and, most importantly, the tribal communities with whom the project would be developed. The Tribal Peace project was intended to work with this infrastructure to create a digital environment for the sharing of tribal cultural, economic, and political information.

The grassroots rethinking of technology that Tribal Peace represents interrogates the languages by which it is designed. This is an example of an *ontological turn*. Just like the internet, the "code" that produces software or hardware is also an assemblage, and can therefore be thought of ontologically in relation to the voices and perspectives of the tribal communities. Thinking ontologically means inquiring into the basis by which we articulate that which we know, the ways in which values and beliefs are brought into being (Srinivasan 2012). That includes how we construct technology.

In 2003, after a year, stakeholders from 15 of the 19 communities were brought together from several collaborative design workshops. The goal was to design the Tribal Peace system for community members to share information as they chose across the reservations. This way of designing systems to support communities' values, knowledge practices, and access protocols is known as a *fluid ontology* approach (Srinivasan 2004, 2006a, 2006b, 2007).

A fluid ontology is a set of classifications and semantic relationships expressed by a group of community members used to design a database, algorithm, or technology interface in a locally appropriate manner. It is created through a consensus-driven process whereby a demographically representative community focus group discusses and reflects upon the collective traditions, practices, values, priorities, and epistemologies they share. Through this process, the group designs a semantic map of key topics and their interrelationships (Srinivasan 2006a; Srinivasan, Enote, Becvar, & Boast 2009; Srinivasan & Huang 2005). Points of collective agreement and disagreement are identified, and links between these are drawn out by community members. The key to this fluidity is that the overall structure of knowledge and design can be revisited at any time. Its fluidity lies in this dynamism as well as its connection to the process of collective reflection.

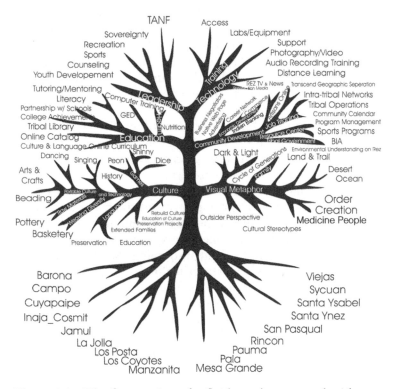

Figure 1.2 The first version of a fluid ontology created with tribal communities across San Diego County

Community members would convene every three months to redesign this ontology based on shifting priorities and points of agreement and disagreement. As figure 1.2 reveals, the initial ontology on which Tribal Peace's databases were structured contained themes that represent historical memory, such as "Ocean," and aspiration for the future, such as "Sovereignty." The communities no longer had any access to the ocean, yet reinserting this theme into the tribal lexicon was important as a means of recovering memory and identity. And while sovereignty, or tribal autonomous governance, remained a politically thorny and little-known issue among the majority of the reservation population, it was a theme to which tribal leaders pledged commitment.

Like the infrastructures that provided the communities with internet access, the fluid ontologies that shaped the Tribal Peace software reveal it as an example of a locally crafted assemblage. The code by which the Tribal Peace system was designed was not created from afar or "customized" for indigenous peoples. Instead, this effort viewed every element of technology as intermingled with not just community members and the places in which they lived, but their values, beliefs, and cosmologies. This is indicated with an interface design based on the metaphor of the Manzanita tree, the restriction of the system to only enrolled tribal members, and the software code and database architectures by which information is represented.

Reflective of Manuel DeLanda's ideas on assemblage theory (DeLanda 2006), the Tribal Peace system was designed by a range of people and places to support the emergence of new leaders, including an 85-year-old medicine woman, a former collegiate football star, and a nationally recognized tribal chairman. These and other individuals, from different reservations and walks of life, came together to take leadership over this effort. The technology was not a surrogate for these physical forms of organizing, or "human networks," but was intended to work with them.

Tribal Peace lives on to this day, now as a system called ACORN, on the servers managed by the tribal chairmen's association on the Pala reservation in Southern California. Like any other effort involving technology, it should not be seen as a panacea or "solution" for the challenges faced by the tribal members of San Diego County. Yet it is an example of how collaboration can shape assemblages that rethink the codes by which technologies are created and what their ultimate significance may be for their creators and users.

The Middle Way: Performing Knowledge and Technology at Zuni

Our ancestors said we should find our truth, our center and middle... and in the process that meant touching other people, engaging other people, and learning from other people...that's why we brought you here, to develop those relationships to build a larger centering, and to develop a search for our truth.

(Jim Enote, October 2014)

With the above words, Jim Enote, Zuni tribal member and director of the A:shiwi A:wan Tribal and Heritage Center in New Mexico, USA, describes the Zuni Native American community's approach toward other peoples, places, and things of the world. Enote explains that the Zuni do not differentiate in their relationships with the external world, whether one speaks of digital technologies or researchers. They view that which is outside of their community with circumspection, to be treated with a respectful distance. This is unsurprising given the centuries of colonization and genocide the Zuni have encountered, including the theft of lands and sacred objects from their community. Yet the Zuni also see themselves as tactical, as occupying a middle way. They recognize that isolation will not benefit their community, and that it may be possible to find "their truth" through interactions with other peoples, places, and things.

Enote and the Zuni have partnered with researchers in an effort devoted to the digital recovery of objects taken from tribal land, and now sitting in the hands of dozens of museums

Figure 1.3 Zuni leadership examining an indigenous map
Source: Ramesh Srinivasan

across the world. Access to digital images of these objects is no substitute for repatriation, or their physical return. Yet, as Enote alludes above, this middle way is not merely about how a technology is used but a larger illustration of what can occur when indigenous values, performances, places, people, and belief systems are brought into interaction with outside organizations and tools. It, like Tribal Peace, is an assemblage in action.

The collaborative effort led by Enote's team is named *Amidolanne*, the Zuni word for rainbow, a metaphor chosen by the Zuni community to describe its approach toward collaboration, intuitively connected to the idea of the "middle way." It relates to the Zuni experience of being interconnected with the world, engaging with a spectrum of objects, people, ideas, and effort. *Amidolanne* has no end, while reaching far and wide in every direction to foster cultural, spiritual, and religious energy.

Amidolanne is also the name of the technology developed by the Zuni. It is a digital and human network, fusing technology-facilitated connections and human relationships. Sharing several hundred digital images of Zuni objects, the effort is dedicated not only to the support of tribal protocols around how knowledge is circulated but also to support the ways it is performed. A Filemaker Pro system, designed collaboratively by researchers and Zuni colleagues, sits at multiple locations on the Zuni pueblo, including the museum Enote directs. External partners, at museums, archives, libraries, and archaeological institutions, are provided access to selected Zuni comments on various objects. These partners have been carefully chosen by the Zuni, an example of how human relationships built on trust and communication can give rise to a digital network, and how technology and culture are inseparable.

Enote's team has worked diligently to clarify the meaning of *Amidolanne*, metaphorically and as a technology, so to appropriately communicate with the larger Zuni community. The system is described with the subtitle: "Supporting authentic Zuni narratives from the source." In a promotional document circulated to the entire pueblo and other stakeholders outside of Zuni, *Amidolanne* has been described as strengthening "Zuni-led and -controlled knowledge sharing in order to sustain Zuni philosophy, language, and arts for generations to come" (December 14, 2012). Enote's team has also clarified that the audiences for this system are primarily local (museum staff, schools, artists, historic preservation office and religious leaders) and secondarily external (subscribing museums, collections institutions, archaeologists, anthropologists, and ethnographers).

Instead of one laptop per user, tribal members would *collectively* use a single computer, which would make images accessible from the *Amidolanne* system via a large screen at the front of the room at the Tribal and Heritage Center in which we gathered (Srinivasan 2012). Tribal members would engage in conversations related to each object they viewed, switching languages at various times.

As Srinivasan (2017) describes in his collaboration with the Zuni, at one point during the collective viewing a younger tribal member who directly interacted with the technology scrolled to an image of a colorful figurine featuring a headdress, shoes, and ornate clothes. The image of this ancient being, an *Anahoho*, activated a lively discussion. The discussion proceeded in the Zuni language, and every several minutes the young facilitator would write notes down in English. During this process, several Zuni youth would either leave the room,

Figure 1.4   Zuni community members collectively viewing digital objects via *Amidolanne*
Source: Ramesh Srinivasan

put their fingers in their ears, or remain silent. After an hour, the discussion concluded.

Why did some young Zuni put their fingers in their ears while we viewed the images of this ancient being? Why did a dozen people view one computer screen? Why were the several laptops in the room left unused, given that each individual could use the system on his or her own? Why was the discussion so lively between the Zuni elders who already knew one another? Why was the Zuni language spoken so often with only small parts of this discussion written into the system, and that too in English? And what demarcated the difference between the speaking and writing of English versus the speaking (and lack of writing) of Zuni?

This moment, consistent with many others, reveals the problems with naïve myths that treat technologies and their uses as somehow separate from the cultural practices, values, environments, and peoples that frame their use and meaning. Indeed, this example is about neither the technology nor the tribal members in isolation, but instead about an assemblage that brings them together. It is an example of what Andrew Pickering (2010) has described as a "mangle of practice." The image of the *Anahoho*, and the technology by which it was presented, played a role in the performing of Zuni knowledge, through the stories that were told and the ways in which individuals present engaged with these. It speaks to the ways in which knowledge emerges for Zuni through conversation and communication. Zuni knowledge is embodied, brought to life through collective performance and conversation.

The *Amidolanne* effort, similar to other examples we share in this chapter, reveals a community-articulated assemblage in practice. Like Tribal Peace, we see a system built upon the ontologies articulated by an indigenous community, in this case the Zuni. Yet in the story of the *Anahoho* we also see a technology interwoven with numerous physical and material elements, most notably the knowledge practices and belief systems of the Zuni. It is an actor within a network of people and other entities that support Zuni ontological life – the rituals, performances, and interactions between different participants. And in that sense, like Tribal Peace, it is an assemblage where technology, culture, place, and people are inseparable.

Lateral Sound: Making the Margins – a New Center in Oaxaca, Mexico

This chapter has described how framings of the digital divide operate under the mistaken presumption that culturally diverse global communities can and should use technology from afar, at times literally in the clouds, to engage with the larger world, for example to communicate with the government, or gain employment from access to online digital labor tasks.

It is important for us to point out that at times "digital divide" projects can add value to user communities. For example, Parminder Singh (2010) has described the internet as a central space for the flow of economic, social, political, cultural capital in his analysis of technology and the digital divide in rural India and other "developing" nations of the global South. Similarly, Andrew Kakabadse and colleagues point to the need for governmental intervention to ensure equitable access to information (Kakabadse, Kakabadse, & Kouzmin 2003).

Yet while this research describes inequality in terms of access to services or institutional accountability, it is also limited in that it fails to consider what is lost when we think of technologies as a vehicle for a particular form of external communication, rather than as part of an assemblage driven *within* a community itself. The examples we have shared reveal the importance of learning from and supporting assemblages that emerge from within a community. They point to the power of developing assemblages between and across communities otherwise framed as silent and objectified users of new technology.

Our final case study describes a partnership underway with leaders of the Rhizomatica initiative in the province of Oaxaca, Mexico. This collaboration between activists, social entrepreneurs, and rural indigenous communities aims to build and support communication and development for people who otherwise lack the resources and expertise to use new technologies to support their economic and political goals. Instead of dropping a technology system or infrastructure "from the sky," Rhizomatica has helped a group of more than 30 communities lobby to access unused frequencies of the mobile telephony spectrum, and set up open-source hardware and software systems for mobile telephony by which they can call one another within and across their communities.

The project works with voice over mobile telephone towers connected to internet protocol (VoIP) technology to make possible oral communication in Zapotec and Mixtec languages within and across participating communities, as well as to those outside of their lands with whom community members may wish to speak. The economic models, infrastructural design, languages spoken, and associated cosmologies of "speaking into the air" reveal Rhizomatica as another example of what may be possible when we think of assemblages involving digital technologies from the perspective of grassroots global communities. Yet it also raises important questions as to what autonomy and sovereignty truly mean when it comes to a community having voice and power over an infrastructure, given that any "new" infrastructure such as mobile telephony is likely to be reliant on other infrastructures to which it is daisy-chained, such as electricity.

The history of telecommunications research has revealed how as technology infrastructures spread to marginal and rural communities, their inclusion of these groups reinforces rather than eradicates their subordinate position. Telecommunications and policy scholar Harmeet Sawhney, for example, has shown across multiple pieces how telephone access in rural communities, even within the United States, supports a system where calls are routed through urban centers (Sawhney 1992a, 1992b, 1992c; Sawhney et al. 1991). The flows of information within networks that claim to decentralize actually work to cement hierarchies of urban privilege that in turn support those with power and wealth. One can apply similar analyses to internet and mobile phone initiatives across the world, and particularly within developing-world or indigenous communities.

These forms of infrastructural marginalization have been discussed by communications scholar James Carey (2002), who articulates the contrast between "transmission" and "ritual" models of communication. The transmission model of communication routes telephone networks through positions and systems of power. In contrast, a ritual approach focuses on network-building *between* communities on the margins, reimagining technology relative to an assemblage that includes values of sharing, collectivity, and fellowship.

There are several notable respects in which Rhizomatica may step away from the transmission model of technology-aided inequality. First, the infrastructural design and economic models involved are *collective*. No individual or institution holds disproportionate power over the financial outcomes of the effort, and all are said to be provided the opportunity to participate equally in the design process. Second, like the two examples we have shared involving Native American communities, this effort places these rural indigenous communities *at the center* of an infrastructure of communication and considers how these tools may support agendas and values from within. Indeed, this insight is consistent with research that has shown, perhaps surprisingly, that the vast majority of calls and emails people send across the world tend to be to others within their own geography rather than far away. Finally, this effort is *oral*, interwoven with Zapotec and Mixtec cosmologies that speak of the value of knowing that is "spoken into the air." Many indigenous languages remain mostly or completely oral within the Oaxaca region, despite the existence of phonetic writing systems developed recently. Yet these languages remain unspoken by many community members, partly due to their exclusion by the Mexican educational system. By working with oral communication via mobile telephony, the Rhizomatica initiative supports existing systems and networks of communication within and across these communities.

Rhizomatica users now have a platform they collectively own by which they can communicate with fellow community members for free, and the opportunity to call users outside of their community for a fraction of the previous price, including making international calls at approximately 1 percent of the former rate. This has shaped the development of several indigenous-led enterprises that have taken advantage of the communication platform to find collaborators, customers, and employees.

The above could not occur simply through providing access to an existing technology or network, but instead rethinking technology relative to assemblages shaped across these Mexican villages. The mobile phone spectrum, inexpensive handsets, community-owned mobile towers, internet-amplifying technology, the mountainous landscapes of rural Oaxaca, and of course indigenous languages and voices – together these components constitute the Rhizomatica assemblage.

Curbing Our Digital Enthusiasm

Tribal Peace, Amidollane, Rhizomatica, and other examples we have shared in this chapter speak to how an assemblage "from below" can contest hierarchy and hegemony. In this spirit, sociologist and philosopher of science David Turnbull has argued that we must not devalue "knowledge," "knowing," "identity," or "being" by clinging to the static models that Deleuze and Guattari are so critical of in their articulation of assemblage theory. Turnbull (2009) thus asks us to rethink the very ideas of assemblage and of diversity in the image of multiplicity, "which implies rethinking our understanding of science and knowledge and of the enlightenment project itself."

This chapter has asked us to listen to and learn from assemblages that fuse community life. We must respect and learn from the belief systems, knowledge practices, infrastructures, environments, and peoples that we work with rather than ignore these. What is at stake in this discussion is not just a question of who uses technology or the spreading of "access." Ultimately, as we rethink the internet in terms of community-based assemblages, we embrace an element of diversity often forgotten by mainstream conversations of technologies and their uses. In working with community-articulated assemblages, an alternative path surfaces toward thinking of our world "after the internet."

2
Hacking the Hacktivists

As this book's introduction discusses, the internet's decentralized architecture presents opportunities for nation-states, data-gathering corporations, and political movements. Yet it also has created opportunities for technology users and activists, who may resist forms of surveillance and tracking, concerned with the amount of data being gathered about citizens across seemingly many aspects of their lives.

The term "hacker" brings together a number of typologies, from "white hat" activists devoted to democratic principles and values to malevolent "black hat" hackers primarily interested in the subversive breaking of laws without a necessary commitment to democratic values. This chapter's interest is in exploring the dialectically related assemblages produced by both states and hacktivists as they engage in their work with digital technology. These assemblages, like the many others we share throughout this book, are not restricted to the internet itself in a closed sense, but instead bring network technologies into a dialogue with a number of other social and technical factors.

To best understand the game of cat and mouse around hacktivism we must see the internet in relation to a number of policing efforts, which place networked technology in a precarious relationship with several legal and technological practices. This chapter's contribution is to illuminate assemblages that are at the center of the hacktivist battle for a free and open internet and the values for which it stands. The assemblages of hacktivism includes *legal statutes*, technologies of *encryption/decryption* that aid and disrupt surveillance, and three key practices employed by both hacktivists and states: *selfie-incrimination*, *versioning*, and *edgework*.

There are a multiplicity of states implicated in this discussion, from neoliberal democracies, such as in parts of Europe and North America, to networked authoritarian states that maintain strong ministries of information. Nonetheless, every nation-state, regardless of its intention or history, is in an interesting position today as it considers how to use digital technology to balance issues such as citizen privacy or civil rights relative to security and the desire to control and know about one's constituencies. This chapter considers how the use of technologies for dissent is shaping legal and policing practices in the United States and United Kingdom and, via their extra-judicial actions, worldwide. We note that though our focus is on neoliberal democracies, one can see battles with hacktivists also relative to a range of authoritarian regimes wishing to control and manipulate information.

Recent Histories of Hacktivism

Chelsea Manning leaked secret military documents to WikiLeaks and was sentenced to 35 years in prison in Fort Leavenworth, Kansas. Jeremy Hammond is currently serving 10 years in a federal prison for hacking and releasing documents about US military subcontractor Stratfor. Aaron Swartz received a felony conviction and was facing a prison sentence of 25 years for hacking documents out of JSTOR (a scholarly article database) when he committed suicide in 2013. While all three are American citizens, and therefore subject to American laws and punishments, the US administration pursues hackers located overseas for alleged criminal activities. Although their tactics are often technically illegal, hacktivists tend to be united by a common belief that it is more important to share information and fight for an internet that is public rather than honor private property or follow what they see as unjust laws.

The decentralized architecture of the internet has been exploited by both states and hackers in their ongoing battle over the control versus liberation of information. The practices of neither, however, demonstrate an acceptance with the internet "as is". Instead both states and hackers exploit the internet's relationship to other technologies that allow for data to be either monitored or authored anonymously. In this sense, the internet is mutable due to being part of an assemblage inclusive of other systems and tools. Thus we see an ongoing battle around technologies to evade and support monitoring – from IP address-scrambling and email encryption to tools that aid surveillance.

Within the United States, practices of dissent such as civil disobedience were defended by the original writers of the US Constitution. Since the attacks of September 11, 2001, and likely as we move forward with the Trump administration, both domestic dissent within the United States and political upheavals outside of the nation have been increasingly labeled as forms of terrorism. Terrorism has emerged as a discourse to be broadly interpreted and acted upon by a range of governmental agencies, corporations, and media networks. The expansion and growth of the internet, via the world wide web and mobile platforms, has thus made it increasingly relevant as a battlefield between the visions of hackers versus the surveillance, digital propaganda, and "anti-terror" initiatives launched by governments and corporations.

Recently a number of hacktivists and communitarian activists have been prosecuted in high-profile court cases. Individuals like Edward Snowden, Julian Assange, Chelsea Manning, Jeremy Hammond, Barrett Brown, Ross Ulbricht, and others are being investigated or have been sentenced to prison. This includes a range of activists who push for governmental transparency and the creation of underground countercultural technology-mediated communities, such as the darknet marketplace Silk Road. The manner in which these hacktivists were investigated, prosecuted, and sentenced reveals the practices of a networked state on the edge of legality, or engaged in *edgework* (Fish & Follis 2015, 2016), practiced by both criminal investigators and hackers.

In this chapter we focus on politically motivated hacktivists of two kinds. The first are *crackers*, computer "geeks" who break into secure systems for the challenge and pleasure, and also in order to bring to the public various forms of information. The second type of hacktivist could be seen as within the lens of *alternative computing*, including those who create illegal systems that are designed to challenge the legitimacy of the state or powerful corporation. The Silk Road is an example of the latter, but so too is WikiLeaks, the publisher of whistleblown information.

Central to the motivation for hacking is the pursuit of information that is often obscure or outright forbidden. For this reason, hacking necessitates a "politics of transgression" (Coleman 2003). This ethic often develops into a morality as it becomes socially adopted and transformed over time. On one level, hackers' technical imaginaries begin with discussions of computers, networks, protocols, and a distaste for proprietary software. On another level, hacker conversations reveal moralities regarding free speech, meritocracy, privacy, openness, and individualism. Hacker "morality" (Coleman & Golub 2008: 267) thus considers principles of selfhood, property, privacy, labor, and creativity for the digital age.

The quintessential hacker WikiLeaks editor Julian Assange has long argued for the importance of maintaining the transparency of the activities of those with power and privilege. He has stated that "the greater the power, the more need there is for transparency, because if the power is abused, the result can be so enormous. On the other hand, those people who do not have power, we mustn't reduce their power even more by making them yet more transparent" (Aitkenhead 2013). Hackers like Assange have seemingly embraced the challenge of "liberating information" to then force the powerful to be accountable for their actions. Like Assange, who is currently holed up on the third floor of the Ecuadorian Embassy in London, the hacktivists discussed in this chapter have been persecuted for their moral and technical imaginaries about how the world should be. While not all hackers, even the ones we highlight in this chapter, are the same in terms of their moral motivations and digital practices, we believe it is useful to identify shared elements whereby they and the systems they fight against incorporate the internet into an assemblage with other elements.

A common interpretation is to see hacktivism as a form of civil disobedience. Civil disobedience has a varied history across the world. In the United States, some scholars have argued for the legality of this form of protest (Calabrese 2004), while others, such as the Metropolitan Police in the United Kingdom (Cluley 2011), warn potential digital protestors of its illegality. Hacktivist civil disobedience is thus an example of liminality, occupying a position that is at both sides of a boundary or threshold. Jürgen Habermas argues that "[t]he 'right' to civil disobedience remains suspended between legitimacy and legality for good reasons. But the constitutional state which prosecutes civil disobedience as a common crime falls under the spell of an authoritarian regime" (1985: 112).

The success of the prosecution, the rate of incarceration, and the draconian sentences handed down to hacktivists challenge the notion that the internet remains a place for transgressive political activism or civil disobedience. It is evidence that public speech in an increasingly digital world can be increasingly used to police, apprehend, and control. For a time online anonymity and pseudoanonymity were not difficult to achieve and with these tools evade prosecution. The assembled nature of the internet, a "heterogeneity of component elements" (Anderson, Kearnes, McFarlane, & Swanton 2012: 174), allowed for hidden spaces and darknets, and thus immunity. At the same time the increased existence of all sectors of society online – government, finance, civil society, private information – also made ripe the conditions for new forms of political activism focused on using computers and networks to open up and publicize otherwise private information, or to subvert systems of political and social power. These tensions between privacy and publicity are inherent in a system of such heterogeneous diversity. Government and corporate forces may push for transparency of citizen users and enemy states, though not for their own activities, as a matter of "national security." In this ideological confrontation, hacktivists are antagonists to the state, and competitors over the information commons. Thus the state has a vested interest in making the opaque conditions of the internet clear by bringing it into the light of law. State agents may attempt to incorporate the internet into an assemblage involving laws and interpretations that can then shape hacktivist persecution. In contrast, hacktivists attempt to develop assemblages around the internet that involve leakages, covert community formations, and pseudoanonymity.

This chapter analyzes hacktivists, how some have been caught, and the underlying ideology of the states that pursued them. We find that in addition to technological and legal elements, the hacktivist–state assemblage must include three extra-judicial practices: (1) *selfie-incrimination*, or self-disclosure on social media that unintentionally empowers surveillance systems; (2) *versioning*, or deliberate uses of technology to deceive one's adversary and therefore make one's identity vague; and (3) *edgework*, or technological or other practices that lie in the zone of liminal legality (Fish & Follis 2015, 2016).

Our conclusion is sobering. Our analyses of these assemblages reveal that the state retains an upper hand by defining the grounds of legality and that its use of non-technological elements such as the manipulation of the legal system (e.g. in the United States) or brutal killing of those who dissent (e.g. in Iran, Egypt, Saudi Arabia, and other countries) has paved the way for a world today where hacktivists are increasingly persecuted. Where this battle goes will in large part shape what type of internet the world will experience moving forward.

The Battle between Agency and Structure

A long-standing concern within social theory has been the relationship between *agency* and *structure* (Bourdieu 1990). In general, theorists have tended to prioritize the importance of one or the other of these as they speculate on the factors that constitute and shape social life. For example, scholars in cultural studies tend to emphasize the creativity, flexibility, and evasiveness of cultural practices, while others, such as functionalists, political economists, and Marxists, often ascribe a constraining or limiting role to individual agency because of the dominance of social and economic institutions (e.g. laws, courts, schools, government bureaucracies, the labor market, etc.). Though these forms of scholarship position agency and structure as oppositional and independent, we believe that an understanding of hacktivism and states must consider agents and the social structures within which they act as mutually constitutive (Giddens 1984).

Classical debates over agency and structure are complicated by the increasingly prominent role played by technology in social life. Here we find a parallel dynamic that maps onto the agency/structure binary. Hackers, for example, tend to argue that the internet embodies sacrosanct principles of freedom and autonomy. This posture is often technologically deterministic and teleological as they point out that the free play of technology and innovation drives history. Criminal investigators and lawmakers, on the other hand, often argue that the internet is a system capable of being regulated and modified in line with dominant social and institutional norms. In other words, they prioritize the social construction and regulation of technology as a necessary constraint on the anarchy of individual autonomy. The inability of the internet to fully support either vision is evidence of its generativity as well as its incompleteness. It speaks to how a far more insightful understanding of this networked technology infrastructure would consider it within an assemblage of other legal, technological, and policing factors and practices.

Following Anthony Giddens' (1984) work on structuration and Bruno Latour's (1996) analyses of scientific knowledge production, we see hacktivists, criminal investigators, and the practices engendered by the internet in a state of co-production. In this sense, the internet is being collectively reassembled via the ongoing battle between hackers and agents of the state. This is consistent with a number of studies, not solely of the internet, but within the larger domain of science and technology itself. For example, Latour (1996) revealed in his ethnographies of laboratories how an older version of elitist top-down science was replaced by a "collective experiment" in which scientists worked with policymakers and the public in forming scientific knowledge. We can look at this chapter's themes with a similar lens.

Relationships between hacktivists and states are not premised on an equal access to power but are rather characterized by inequality, friction, and conflict. Anna Tsing, in her ethnography of the relationships between environmentalists, indigenous people, and illegal loggers, identified the spaces where these actors meet as "zone[s] of awkward engagement" shaped by *friction* and the "awkward, unequal, unstable, and creative qualities of interconnections across difference" (2005:

4). These interconnections "remind us that heterogeneous and unequal encounters can lead to new arrangements of culture and power" (2005: 6). In this sense, the ways agents of the state and hacktivists reassemble the internet are relative to historical and ongoing relationships of power inequity. On the one hand, states use their immense technical and legal resources in order to create "lines of sight" that transect the internet, attempting to create new forms of visibility. Yet on the other, hacktivists have a moral interest in supporting privacy and evasion of surveillance.

Despite ongoing state initiatives to spy on, monitor, regulate, and control the "space" of the internet, it is not a terrain dominated by the state (indeed the reverse is in some respects the case). The state's tactics thus must involve reading and mapping the quickly shifting terrain of online interaction until openings appear in the hacktivist community that bring particular targets within its line of sight. It is here that the state can bring to bear its particular strategic advantage by proceeding under the mantle of its offline home terrain: its ability to exploit legal and policing factors.

The above is to say that until investigators are able to move proceedings offline, the state must approach the "space" of the internet much in the same way as hackers approach the terrain of the state. Both adversaries must be nimble, flexible, and mobile: their reassembled internets are configured by the tactics used to support their agendas and debilitate their adversaries. They must be nomadic, in essence defying what Gilles Deleuze and Félix Guattari (1987) have described as the "war machine" of the traditional state. Yet in the past nation-states have often not been able to appropriate the tactics of their nomadic adversaries owing to their bureaucratic histories and forms of structural overhead. All of that shifted in the Western world in the late 20th century, as we now describe.

Netwar

According to one classical definition, the state is an organization that successfully monopolizes the means of legitimate violence in a given territory (Weber 1946: 78). In this view,

a state is primarily defined through its institutional bureaucratic structure, its capacity to penetrate and organize social
relations through institutions, as well as its instrumental use
of violence and coercion to maintain authority (Mann 2012).
Toward the end of the 20th century, this "Westphalian" model
of the sovereign state (as autonomous and supreme within its
territorial boundaries) was said to undergo a process of "down-
sizing" as a result of the combined pressures of the information
age and globalization (Castells 1996). For a number of com-
mentators writing in the 1990s, the scale of international
cross-border flows, as well as the increasing global prominence
of international organizations, multinational corporations, and
other non-state actors, pointed to an eclipse or "withering"
of the state on the global stage (Reich 1991).

However, the late 20th and early 21st centuries witnessed
a dramatic expansion of the nation-state's punitive, repressive,
and covert activities across the world, particularly within
Western Europe and North America. The events of 9/11 and
the ensuing Global War on Terror systematically eroded or
blurred previously held distinctions between matters of external
and internal security (i.e. the distinctions between war and
crime, military and police, detention and imprisonment) (Bigo
2000). Discourses of terror, or, if you will, "shock doctrines,"
helped pave the way for this erosion of civil liberties and relative anonymity not just in the physical world but also in the
relationship of citizen users with internet technologies.

These dynamics mark the origins of the "networked state."
Key insights into this concept come from the work of David
Ronfeldt and John Arquilla, collaborators at the US military-
funded think-tank the RAND Corporation. Ronfeldt is a senior
social scientist at RAND and Arquilla is a RAND consultant
and professor of defense analysis at the Naval Postgraduate
School. Their research on networked war ("netwar") and the
networked military state ("counternetwar") draws from the
sociology of networks and activism and is intended to inform
the US military about how best to combat technology-facilitated
terrorists, revolutionaries, and activists. Today, their ideas are
operationalized against hacktivists, which may fall into any
of these three categories as far as the state is concerned.

Whilst writing the papers analyzed below, Arquilla advised
the office of Donald Rumsfeld, the Secretary of Defense under

George W. Bush. A supporter of preemptive war, aggressive cyber-attacks, and National Security Agency (NSA) wiretapping, Arquilla (2013) has argued for the importance of big data to "search out small cells that bedevil our era." These "small cells" include "peaceful social activists," Zapatista indigenous activists in rural Mexico, "malcontents, ne'er-do-wells," and "anarchist and nihilistic leagues of computer-hacking 'cyboteurs'." On the "bright side" are the "good guys" like RAND, the US Army, and the police state (Ronfeldt & Arquilla 2001: 2–3). In a sense, Arquilla's work supports the networked state to engage in efforts to root out and subvert the tactics of not just hacktivists but any form of opposition that takes on a networked form. Arquilla, Ronfeldt, and their colleagues at RAND recommend that the US military and state-based police and surveillance institutions restructure around the model of the network in order to respond to "adversaries" in the information age.

Beginning in 1993, these scholars began to define "netwar" to "refer to the emerging mode of conflict (and crime) at societal levels, short of traditional military warfare, in which the protagonists use network forms of organization and related doctrines, strategies, and technologies attuned to the information age" (Ronfeldt & Arquilla 2001: 3). Netwar is made possible by the proliferation of networked technologies which enable small groups or cells to organize and "swarm" in their coordinate attacks, an "amorphous, but deliberately structured, coordinated, strategic way to strike from all directions at a particular point or points, by means of a sustainable pulsing of force and/or fire" (Ronfeldt & Arquilla 2001: 12).

The recommendation from RAND to the US military is that governmental agencies should organize themselves in cell-like structures, so that they may more dynamically share information and be able to swarm upon targets. It is important that the state not abandon hierarchy entirely but blend hierarchies and networked organizational structures. In his study of post-Soviet economies, sociologist David Stark (2009) calls these mixed hierarchies and horizontalities *heterarchies*. The US Counterterrorist Center at the CIA is a good example of an adaptive heterarchy. The Israeli Defense Forces (IDF), likewise influenced by information theory, are also adopting a cell-based swarm approach to battle. In terms they appropriated from

Deleuze and Guattari, they have encouraged their soldiers to theoretically "deterritorialize" the urban fabric and literally "walk through walls" in order to apprehend the Palestinian opposition (Weizman 2007: 185).

Heterarchy is thus not merely a philosophical structure or formation but interwoven with three factors or practices that characterize the assemblages associated with the internet in an ongoing battle between the networked state and hacktivists. To spell this out further, we describe *selfie-incrimination*, *versioning*, and *edgework*.

Selfie-incrimination

Every day, it seems, another hack or leak occurs. In June 2015, Chinese hackers were able to gain access to the US Office of Personnel Management (OPM), acquiring the personal data of 4.10 million former and current employees (Nakashima 2015). The FBI says the leak was bigger, containing data from 18 million people (Perez & Prokupecz 2015). Yet when the US NSA and Chinese hackers are not exfiltrating personal information, technology users are voluntarily providing it to private Silicon Valley corporations, whose security is not always stellar. The users are being hacked themselves by consenting to have their data opened up for corporate monetization and political surveillance, often by signing onto bureaucratic and obfuscating terms of service.

One billion gigabytes are currently stored in data centers, the same as 67 million iPhones (Holt & Vonderau 2015). Every day, 350 million photos are uploaded to Facebook. Social media has become the platform for self-expression. The use of the word "selfie" increasing by 17,000 percent in 2013 and 50 percent of the photos on Instagram in the UK by 14- to 21-year-olds are self-portraits. We are thus living in an "infoglut" constituted by an abundance of self-expression (Andrejevic 2013), which in turn gives rise to "selfie-incrimination" when those deemed as criminals wilfully self-expose online.

Cynics see digital self-expressivity as narcissistic (Keen 2015), while, in contrast, optimists witness in the selfie craze the seeds of personal and community empowerment (Nemer & Freeman 2015). Regardless of the academic debate, law enforcement personnel are increasingly using social media to generate evidence and support policing activity (Risen & Poitras 2014). A recent US-based study concluded that 80 percent of investigators searched online for information about suspects (Zadrozny 2015). As a sergeant from an Arizona police force stated, "I think social media used properly could really be a very good tool to help us do our job and really cheap because it doesn't cost anything" (Fox10 2011).

At times, hacktivists themselves fall prey to the desire for self-expression. The most absurd case is that of Higinio O. Ochoa III, an associate of Anonymous. After cracking and releasing Arizona police officers' addresses and phone numbers, Ochoa proceeded to post a tweet linked to these documents under the Twitter handle @Anonw0rmer. Associated with the tweet was an image of Ochoa's girlfriend's breasts above a sign bragging about the stunt. Yet unfortunately for Ochoa, the image contained geolocatable metadata leading to his arrest (Diaz 2012) (figure 2.1).

In another example, selfie-incrimination played an integral role in identifying Ross Ulbricht, aka Dread Pirate Roberts, the "kingpin" of the online drug platform the Silk Road. On his LinkedIn page, Ulbricht described his work as "creating an economic simulation to give people a first-hand experience of what it would be like to live in a world without the systemic use of force" (figure 2.2). Ulbricht used his real name on a coder site to ask, "How can I connect to a Tor hidden service using curl in php?" "Curl" is the code used on Silk Road's web servers. Ulbricht's capture was the result of these breaches of private information on public networks, leading to his apprehension and a brutal sentence of life imprisonment.

Online platforms, while useful for personal communications, also thus assist criminal investigations. This is self-incrimination in action. Online platforms also can deceive through the use of fake profiles and misinformation. On the policing side, new skills of criminal investigation are needed, such as the investigator's knowledge of software code. Such expertise would allow a technical question asked by Ulbricht on the Stack Overflow forum to be linked to the underlying

Kylie Ochoa
@MissAnonFatale

Follow

@LuvLulzSex @Anonw0rmer @DollFoSho
@VizFoSho Mum shows this

PwNd by
w0rmer & CabinCr3w
<3 u BiTch's !

RETWEETS   LIKES
3   2

10:42 am - 11 Mar 2012

2   3   2

Figure 2.1   Higinio O. Ochoa III's selfie-incrimination

technical architecture of the Silk Road platform. Thus, investigators need to shift their practices and formations in accor-
dance with the netwar position we have described. Such
evidence may not always be intentionally "'selfie"-based, but
gathered inductively through a suspect's online activity across
multiple digital platforms. Data aggregation and retention are

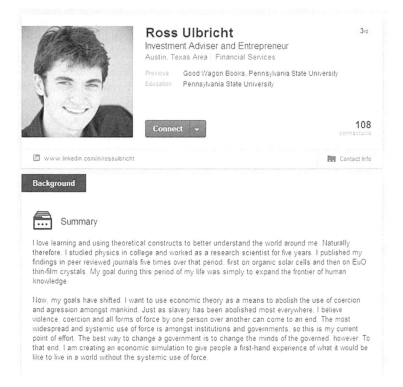

Ross Ulbricht 3rd

Investment Adviser and Entrepreneur

Austin, Texas Area | Financial Services

Previous   Good Wagon Books, Pennsylvania State University
Education   Pennsylvania State University

Connect ▾

108
connections

www.linkedin.com/in/rossulbricht   Contact Info

Background

Summary

I love learning and using theoretical constructs to better understand the world around me. Naturally therefore, I studied physics in college and worked as a research scientist for five years. I published my findings in peer reviewed journals five times over that period, first on organic solar cells and then on EuO thin-film crystals. My goal during this period of my life was simply to expand the frontier of human knowledge.

Now, my goals have shifted. I want to use economic theory as a means to abolish the use of coercion and agression amongst mankind. Just as slavery has been abolished most everywhere, I believe violence, coercion and all forms of force by one person over another can come to an end. The most widespread and systemic use of force is amongst institutions and governments, so this is my current point of effort. The best way to change a government is to change the minds of the governed, however. To that end, I am creating an economic simulation to give people a first-hand experience of what it would be like to live in a world without the systemic use of force.

Figure 2.2   Ross Ulbricht's LinkedIn page

thus key in piecing together information garnered from selfie-incrimination.

One notable exception to selfie-incrimination might be the "semi-naked" (Coleman 2014: 183) hacktivist Barrett Brown, a freelance journalist who had written for *Vanity Fair*, the *Huffington Post*, and the *Guardian*. Though prosecutors originally charged Brown with ten counts of aggravated identity theft and two counts of credit card fraud for posting an HTTP link to leaked emails from Stratfor, these charges were eventually dropped when he pleaded guilty to the crimes of accessory, obstruction, and threatening a federal officer in exchange for a deal. Unlike other cases of selfie-incrimination, Brown attempted to take on a journalistic identity as a Constitutional shield. And ultimately it was his publicity that made him an easy target. Being a cyber-activist with a link to a battery of controversial files and contacts in the journalistic community made him even more visible.

While it is unsurprising that an important step in an investigation is a Google search of a suspect's personal details, it is important to note how social media evidence is admissible in affidavits and other court documents. This is an example of how social media activity combined with legal statutes can contribute to an assemblage shaped by police and security forces.

In the past, states went to extensive lengths to make their populations legible and readable; state interventions in society (e.g. vaccination campaigns, conscription of soldiers) required the creation of "visible" units that could then be observed, identified, monitored, or manipulated (Scott 1998: 183–4). In "seeing like a state" (Scott 1998), citizens and constituencies could be classified and quantified, allowing them to be calculated and monitored to support how resources are distributed. One can view the history of citizen databases, lists, and census data in such a manner. Yet instead of gathering information through formal mechanisms of requesting citizen input, states can monitor the social media activity of their citizens to make them intimately legible. What is crucial here is not just that social media *per se* are premised upon visibility but that the legibility of individuals is a basic embedded component of online interaction. The lack of understanding around how citizen users are made legible through the monitoring of their data increases the likelihood of selfie-incrimination.

Versioning

A second theme to be considered around the hacktivist assemblage is *versioning*. The practice of versioning emphasizes the portabililty, process orientation, and performativity of software culture. Anonymity, pseudoanonymity, privacy, and secrecy may all be pursued in online spaces that do not have "real name" policies, such as Facebook. Despite the fact that users of social media accidentally or purposely deposit digital artifacts (geolocation, IP logs, cookies) that can be traced back to individual users, some social media platforms continue to be spaces for identity performance. We introduce the term "versioning" in order to discuss how hackers' and criminal investigators' identities are mutable. This reflects the mirror image of selfie-incrimination, as it facilitates the ability to evade apprehension.

The ability to be anonymous online has increasingly resulted in the development of a culture of shifting identities. As we have alluded to, hacker culture contrasts greatly to the fixed way by which the state has traditionally seen identity and its linkages to textual evidence. The state has traditionally tended to identify its constituencies as sets of static identities, while the slipperiness of hacker identity speaks to a different mode of performance (Butler 1997). Hackers, in this sense, are postmodern; they are skeptical about the links between identity and what is said online. In this way, hacker culture personifies postmodern linguistics, whereby the signifier is disconnected from the signified (Derrida 1978). The clash over versioned identities represents a major flashpoint in the battles between hacktivists and states.

As our previous discussions of netwar suggest, cybercrime investigators increasingly use hacker practices and values. This involves entering into online spaces where hackers discuss their work, such as internet relay chat (IRC) rooms. To better aid their success, undercover cybercrime investigators may also perform versions of themselves in the pursuit of hackers. It is in this manner that versioning represents an important practice that must be considered when we think of the hacktivist assemblage.

The Silk Road case reveals how the pliability of identity is used both in investigations and in criminal acts. US Drug Enforcement Agency Special Agent Carl Force was employed in an undercover role in the Silk Road case, infiltrating Ulbricht, and posting under a number of fake names. But according to Tigran Gambaryan, special agent with the criminal investigation division of the Internal Revenue Service, his work was not only for the state but also for himself. In a statement, the Department of Justice described how Force, "without authority, developed additional online personas and engaged in a broad range of illegal activities calculated to bring him personal

financial gain" (Department of Justice 2015). Force allegedly
took hundreds of thousands of dollars in the form of the
anonymous currency bitcoin destined for the Silk Road and
deposited this in his own personal bitcoin wallet. Using as
many as three pseudonyms, he was accused of wire fraud,
money laundering, and falsifying government documents before
being convicted and sentenced to 78 months in prison in 2015.

Yet another agent investigating the Silk Road was US Secret
Service Special Agent Shaun W. Bridges. Much like Force,
Bridges supplemented his undercover work with the development of "additional online personas and engaged in a broad
range of illegal activities calculated to bring him personal
financial gain" (US District Court for the Northern District
of California 2015). According to a criminal complaint filed
against Force and Bridges, the latter stole $20,000 in the form
of bitcoins from the drugs marketplace after gaining control
of a Silk Road customer representative's account. Bridges then
liquidated the bitcoins for $820,000 and deposited the sum
in a personal investment account. Although seemingly empowered by their supposedly versioned anonymity, both Force and
Bridges – much like the hacktivists discussed above – were
victims of their own selfie-incrimination, with Bridges being
sentenced to 71 months in jail in 2015 (Farivar 2015). In this
sense, loose or careless versioning can quickly transition into
selfie-incrimination.

Versioning, like selfie-identification, thus represents a critical snapshot of how two visions of a fragmented and generative – and, some may say, "broken" – internet contest one
another. Fluidity, a natural state of the postmodern digital
culture of hacktivists, intuitively blends well with an ever-
changing landscape of software and technology. We think
of platforms such as Facebook or Twitter as stable, yet with
deeper scrutiny recognize that they, like other technologies,
are shifting and mutable.

State agents have accordingly had to embrace such a dynamic
techno-versioning culture in their networked organization
structure, surveillance and apprehension practices, and attempts
to manipulate judicial and policing systems. Yet how can the
legal system, based on historical precedent and tradition, be
versioned to make possible the reassembled internet that the
state seeks? The answer is discussed around the concept of

edgework, the third and final component we identify as we think about assemblages of hacktivism and the state.

Edgework

Network theory has come to be a nearly ubiquitous linguistic and analytic approach toward understanding the social impacts and effects of internet and new technology use. In social network analysis, which as a structural analysis of social relations that existed many years before the advent of digital networked communications, individuals or entities are identified as nodes that then may intersect with others as demarcated by links.

In a network, the lines that link one node to only a single other are considered peripheral, or the *edge* of the network. They may be seen as less relevant or central in the ability to understand a sociotechnical phenomenon, and therefore unimportant in an analysis of the internet.

Perhaps surprisingly, however, the practice of surveying the edges of a network – and guarding its boundaries – is important for both internet and social media technology companies. For example, *edgerank* is the name Facebook gave to the algorithm that suggests supposedly relevant content on its news feed. Facebook's algorithm attempts to connect the separate nodes in what CEO and founder Mark Zuckerberg calls the "social graph," or the realm of all possible person-to-person connections. These algorithms make "ordering" decisions on relevance, yet how these decisions are made, including their epistemological bases, remains mostly invisible. While Facebook monitors and curates the social graph of each of its users, its methods remain mostly secret.

Not only are the edges of the network important on a commercial and technical level, but they are also essential in understanding the cat and mouse game of hacktivism and policing. Edgework, which synthesizes the concept of the edge from network theory and ideas from cultural criminology that emphasizes the powers of transgressing boundaries (Lyng 2005; Lyng & Matthews 2007), can be used to describe the way cybercriminal investigation explores the extremities of the social graph and articulates what is legible and legal. In doing edgework, cybercrime investigators approach and appropriate methods from those already on the margins of legality. In attempting to transform the opaque into the transparent, and the anonymous into the identifiable, criminal investigators use edgework as a practice to fix and read a fluid and dynamic online world. Criminal investigators are making the unique cultures the internet encouraged through versioning and self-expression less legal and more vulnerable for policing and prosecution.

While they do this, criminal investigators skirt the edges of legality. As stated by James Chaparro, former Assistant Director for Intelligence for US Immigration and Customs Enforcement:

> There is always this balance of trying to be forward leaning in your investigative techniques and making sure you don't trample on rights at the same time. You want to stay well within the bounds of your legal authority because if you step over the line the evidence is going to be tossed, it isn't going to be admissible in court and you may wind up jeopardizing the outcome of an entire investigation. And so what I think agencies will try to do is they will want to step right up to the line, maybe get a little bit of chalk on their toes, but don't step over it. (Winter 2015)

Social media companies, criminal investigators, and hacktivists patrol the edges of the network, uncovering and translating otherwise private information and identities into public documents. This competition for resources has these actors at odds with each other and at other times as strange bedfellows. According to Julian Assange (2014), all three "collect a vast amount of information about people, store it, integrate it and use it to predict individual and group behaviour."

States, however, have tactics not available to hackers, namely the criminal justice system and greater financial and infrastructural resources with which to improve their position (Fish & Follis 2015, 2016). Through its edgework practices, the state may seek to curtail that which hackers see as a digital commons. Indeed, through the criminal justice system, "governments and corporations seek to erase the antagonistic history of the Internet, rewrite its rules to favor market and corporate activity, and marginalize public goods online in favor of private property and commercial interests" (Beyer & McKelvey 2015: 892).). Thus, the race to uncover incriminating information as well as the battle to defend it through encryption have come to constitute the ever-receding *edges* of the internet and social media.

"Pushing the Boundaries" with the NSA and GCHQ

Considering selfie-incrimination, versioning, and edgework as factors to be considered in relation to technical, policing, and legal elements within the hacktivist–state assemblage, we now consider what these mean together in relation to a major contemporary hacktivism case.

We wish to explore what the documents released by Edward Snowden reveal about the methods of the networked state. Using the Snowden Surveillance Archive (SSA), which has digitized and made searchable all of the documents thus far revealed by Snowden, we were able to critically analyze documents containing key search terms such "hacktivism" and the hacktivist collective "Anonymous" and cross-reference these terms with NSA and GCHQ (Government Communications Headquarters) programs such as ROLLING THUNDER and divisions such as the UK's Joint Threat Research Intelligence Group (JTRIG), which targets hacktivists. The Snowden documents provide supportive insights into how selfie-incrimination, versioning, and edgework converge. These explorations and provocations of criminality reveal the extent to which the security state apparatus has targeted hacktivism as an excuse for dominating otherwise opaque areas of the internet.

A vivid example of the networked state's convergent uses of versioning and edgework is JTRIG, a section of the UK's GCHQ, the British partner in the Five Eyes global intelligence alliance focused on monitoring internet and telecommunication signals. JTRIG has the capacity for computer network attacks (CNA) and computer network information operations (CNIO). Their mission is described as to "Destroy, Deny, Degrade, Disrupt, Deceive and Protect" (The Intercept 2014:

slide 2). In a slide that features the logos of Twitter, flickr, YouTube, and Facebook, CNIO describes its mission as "propaganda, deception, mass messaging, pushing stories, alias development, and psychology" (The Intercept 2014: slide 4). It outlines its capacities for "disruption," including "masquerades, spoofing, [and] Denial of service" on phones, emails, computers, and faxes (figure 2.3). And finally, in another top secret document, JTRIG describes its "hacking process" under the acronym RICE for "(R)econnaissance, (I)nfection, (C)ommand and Control, and (E)xfiltration" (Kirsch et al. 2014: slide 10). Other documents mentioning JTRIG illustrate the unit's capacity to decrypt and de-anonymize The Onion Router (TOR), essentially an anonymizing browser system.

The network state monitors and learns from hackers and in the process explores the edges of legality. To do this it needs to go undercover in IRC chat rooms and closely watch hacker blogs. For instance, the INTOLERANT program enables the NSA to collect the emails of targets already hacked by hackers (NSA 2010). The program LOVELY HORSE directs agents to follow Twitter, IRC chat rooms, and more in order to

UK TOP SECRET STRAP1

Disruption / CNA

- Masquerades
- Spoofing
- Denial of service
  - Phones
  - Emails
  - Computers
  - Faxes

Figure 2.3 GCHQ's JTRIG computer network attacks (CNA)

monitor information activists and security researchers (LOVELY HORSE n.d.). Examples of Twitter accounts worthy of surveillance include several associated with Anonymous and WikiLeaks (Greenwald 2014). With these disruption and surveillance programs, the internet, far from being conducive for digital civil disobedience, is increasingly depoliticized in relation to social movements.

JTRIG is involved in secret online operations, including the infiltration and manipulation of targets' communications. The techniques include "false flag operations," fake victim blog posts, and the posting of negative information online with the goal being the use of social science and other methods to destroy the reputation of targets (JTRIG n.d.). These techniques are used "in lieu of 'traditional law enforcement' against people suspected (but not charged or convicted) of ordinary crimes, or more broadly still, 'hacktivism', meaning those who use online protest activity for political ends" (Greenwald 2014). The edginess of this work is not lost on the GCHQ, which titles a slide "Cyber Offsensive [*sic*] Session: Pushing the Boundaries and Action Against Hacktivism." Here JTRIG admits that it is on the *offensive* and *pushing* the *boundaries* by targeting people neither charged nor convicted and using techniques on the edge of legality.

WikiLeaks, the Pirate Bay, and Anonymous have all been targets of the NSA and GCHQ (Courage Foundation n.d.). For example, when a query was posed to a formerly classified NSA wiki, "Is it OK to target the foreign actors of a loosely coupled group of hackers...such as with Anonymous?", the response was: "As long as they are foreign citizens." This and other exchanges provide a detailed and compelling vantage point from which to see how the state works at the edges of technology and legality in an expanded pursuit of hacktivists. In these documents the NSA can be seen as a brazen – almost rogue – agency capable of writing its own rules as it explores the edges of legality and technicality (Greenwald & Gallagher 2014). In these programs, individuals associated with WikiLeaks, the Pirate Bay, and Anonymous who have not been formally charged with or convicted of anything are nonetheless targeted for surveillance, disruption, and prosecution.

In the above-mentioned ROLLING THUNDER program, GCHQ's JTRIG used a distributed denial of service attack (DDoS) – a way of coordinating multiple computers to flood a site with requests and shut it down in the process – to close an Anonymous server hosting an IRC chat room (Hacktivism: Online Covert Action 2012; Schone, Esposito, Cole, & Greenwald 2014). An NSA slide titled "DDOS" is followed by a transcript from an IRC chat room, within which a user says, "We're being hit by a syn flood. I didn't know whether to quit last night, because of the DDOS." Such a DDoS likely compromised any other websites hosted on that server, silencing the freedom of speech of innocent users of the same server in the process. Scholars believe that hacktivists such as the PayPal 14, who were convicted of conducting a DDoS campaign in support of WikiLeaks, should be protected under the First Amendment of the US Constitution (Greenwald 2014; Leiderman 2013; Sauter 2014). According to this progressive interpretation, DDoS is a virtual sit-in and should be seen as an exercise in freedom of speech and freedom of assembly. However, when exercised by hacktivists, it is seen as an illegal affront to private property, although when used by the NSA, it is as something worth boasting about at a professional conference.

The appropriation of DDoS from its hacktivist roots thus represents a "(re)militarization of the internet" according to Molly Sauter (2014: 145). She writes, "[T]he use of these tactics in the name of law enforcement and national security is a deliberate move to extend the Hobbesian state monopoly on force to include code.... [E]xpansive definitions of what counts as 'weaponized code' or 'cyberweapons' could result in the widespread classification of civilians as 'cyberterrorists or enemy combatants" (Sauter 2014: 148).

The efforts by the cybersecurity divisions of the US and the UK reframe free speech, freedom of assembly, and civil disobedience as criminal activity, revealing how edgework and the judicial and policing systems shape assemblages that threaten the very basis of hacktivism.

Discussion

Versioning, selfie-incrimination, and edgework represent three important flashpoints in the ongoing battle over the form and meaning of the internet. They are critical points that shape and inform the assemblage that links the worlds of hacktivism and the state. They reveal how the internet fails to exist in a pristine vacuum but is instead interwoven within an assemblage of technical, legal, and policing practices and factors. The battle fought between hacktivists and state agents speaks to the historical amnesia each has, with their assumption that a decentralized networked architecture would enhance, respectively, either freedom, autonomy, and radical sovereignty or citizenship, legibility, and disciplining.

We spoke with former FBI agent Chris Tarbell, the man responsible for catching the hacker Sabu and turning him into an informant and also contributing to the arrest of Silk Road founder Ross Ulbricht. He described the near impossibility of avoiding self-incrimination.

> Perfect anonymity is kind of like perfect communism. It sounds ideal but it's really tough. You'd have to have a computer that you never touch any of your social media, any of your bank accounts, you'd have to pay for it through an anonymous payment system like bitcoins or something like that. You know when you get going, let's say I've observed people hacking into things, once they get going they kind of forget some of the stuff, they get excited about what they have broken into. They make that one mistake. Like a robber taking a glove off in the house to pick up the jewels he accidentally touches the door and there's his fingerprint. You know…one simple mistake.

According to Tarbell, to evade selfie-incrimination, hacktivists would need to engage with a deeply fragmented internet, one in which the computers themselves are not networked. Encryption in itself is not enough, nor is versioning. We must thus ask whether any assemblage involving the internet could ever aid the cause of hacktivism, and if so what that might look like. Are we truly in a post-privacy world? And if so, what types of public activity are safe?

What is needed from the perspective of the hacktivists is the reassembly of an internet around principles and practices of encryption, mesh networks, and other technical and legal factors and practices. For them, the internet needs to be demilitarized and extracted from the discourse of securitization, which positions the communication system as a subject of the networked security state rather than as a space that is more radically democratic. Perhaps such an outcome will be facilitated if hacktivists themselves shift their use of rhetoric and symbolism, stepping away from the increasingly ominous and threatening "macrosecuritizing" discourse – which situates their work in the language of global war (Fish 2017a). What we do know is that the future of the internet will be shaped through antagonistic relationships and assemblages between hacktivists and states.

3
Media Activism: Shaping Online and Offline Networks

From the introduction onward, this book has discussed the power of myths in relation to the internet. As "the creative and symbolic dimension of the social world...through which human beings create their ways of living together and their ways of representing their collective life" (Adelman 1989: 83), myths have fueled the mistaken treatment of the internet as static, singular, immersive, and transcendent. When we subscribe to such myths, we may in turn lose our ability to see the internet as an assemblage, inseparable from peoples, places, laws, and environments. The two previous chapters have been devoted to revealing the assemblages within which internet technology is interwoven, from our discussion of the belief systems and environments of indigenous and cross-cultural communities to the legal systems and policing practices that afflict hacktivists.

This chapter takes aim at the internet and its relationship to political activism and revolutions. It considers fieldwork conducted in Egypt and the Occupy movement, as well as the important protests of the Indignados of Spain and the Chilean student movement. Its primary focus on the Arab Spring is all the more important given how the Middle East continues to be a region of great concern and misunderstanding. By showing how the internet's networks are refracted alongside activist assemblages of offline tools and environments, this chapter argues that we must do away with a narrative where

Silicon Valley supplants Cairo in our understanding of political events in Egypt and the Middle East more largely. The insights we share speak to the power of creativity and intuition in the fight for social and political justice. What we propose here is that the internet and digital networks be seen as part of an assemblage that brings together *offline networks and spaces*, *"older" media* such as television and radio, *economic and political institutions*, and *physical bodies* in shaping political activism.

Facebook Revolution?

In June 2011, the shirt pictured in figure 3.1 was purchased in Tahrir Square. Around central Cairo, Ramesh Srinivasan asked Egyptians about the story that it told. "We thank Facebook for our revolution," a subsistence laborer from Giza told him while asking for him to let Facebook know that "we

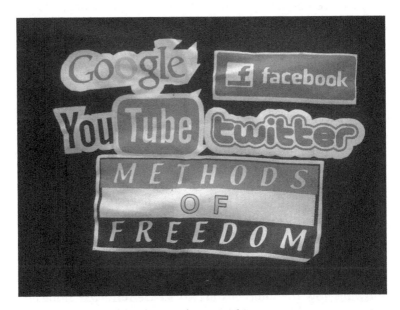

Figure 3.1 Social media revolution t-shirt
Source: Ramesh Srinivasan.

need their help to organize our next government." Ramesh then asked whether he or anyone in his family or neighborhood had internet access at the time of the 18 days of revolution in January/February 2011 and was given the simple answer of "nobody."

This photo reveals an internet-centric explanation of a revolution in action, one that sees technology as the cause of social and political events despite the reality that the Arab Spring revolutionaries alleged to be behind these were mostly disconnected from the internet. Our story of the t-shirt and Tahrir Square demonstrates how a technology-centric explanation of the Arab Spring had not only reached the Western world but also had implanted itself on the streets of Cairo. Yet how could such a narrative be possible given that social media technologies were accessed in fewer than 5 percent of Egyptian homes in early 2011? Would it not be absurd to assume such tools caused a revolution in a country of 85 million?

> They could not believe that we could [start a revolution] so the Western world had to pretend as if it was their tools that liberated us.

Surprisingly, these words were uttered not by a cyber-skeptic such as Malcolm Gladwell but by Gigi Ibrahim (personal conversation, 2015), an Egyptian activist who has over 140,000 Twitter followers, and at the age of 23 was featured on the cover of *Time* (in February 2012) and lionized in *Vanity Fair* (April 2011) as part of the "generation changing the world." These articles (among many others) praise Ibrahim's ability to reach the masses, to rally her fellow Egyptians, and to make democracy possible, supposedly thanks to the social media technologies of the day.

Yet Ibrahim, in conversations with us, defies the "social media revolutionary" label with which she has been identified. She has explained that this pigeonholed identity objectifies her agency and capacity. It emphasizes technology and views her as its accessory. It simplifies the struggles for social and economic justice for which people across the Arab world fight, and ignores the creativity, intuition, humanity, and history behind the social movements of the Arab Spring.

Fetishizing technology runs the risk of ignoring a great deal of research that has studied why and how people protest. It fails to consider the importance of existing political and media climates (McAdam 1982), and the role of symbolic, material, organizational, political, and cultural capacities in shaping protests (Meyer & Minkoff 2004). While prominent sociologists such as Charles Tilly (1990) have written about the importance of "political opportunity" in impacting the sustainability of a social movement, others (Emirbayer 1997; Goodwin & Jasper 1999) write about the power of emotions, agency, and political activism in shaping revolutions. These important factors may be erased from our understanding and appreciation of political movements if we only think about the internet in naïve isolation.

In our introduction, we challenged the myth of the internet as a public space. In this chapter we take aim at another myth, that of the "social media revolution," a framing which reduces the creativity, practices, and imaginaries of protesters into an obsession with internet technologies. Retweeting does not necessarily shape social change, and clicking on an online petition may better represent disengagement rather than stand for a means of fighting injustice (Melber 2011; Morozov 2011). On top of this, Facebook, Twitter, and Google are hardly open – they are in reality slaves to their controlling algorithms and corporate political economies, and only operate on the networks and information that are part of users' lives. Our online friends may be more similar than not to ourselves in real life because of mutual friendship, the places where they live, the interests they have, and their political leanings. And in cases where activists learn from one another online, it is inappropriate to give the technology credit in lieu of understanding the actions of its users. It is all too easy to forget that activists learned from one another before social media existed.

That said, even in countries of the Arab Spring, such as Tunisia, Egypt, or Morocco, where internet access is limited (with numbers even smaller for social media accounts), the presence of digital technologies should not be completely discounted. A technology may be shaped, mediated, and modified. Social media technologies may thus be domesticated (Silverstone & Haddon 1996), appropriated (Jenkins 2006), subverted (Hebdige 1984), and reconstructed.

It is important to respect the dynamic assemblages produced by activists as they struggle to achieve change. The literature we review in this chapter, and the ethnographies we share from Egypt, reveal examples of how activists tactically use a range of different tools, including new technologies, to shape their agenda and reach a range of audiences. Thus while we cannot simply assume that YouTube is a democratizing technology, we can view it as one system amongst many that can assist a movement.

Philosopher Henri Bergson has written about the importance of recognizing and respecting the agency of peoples and communities, consistent with our argument to pay attention to the creativity of activists rather than naïvely praise existing tools and systems. Bergson writes persuasively about the power of intuition, which shapes the poetic experience of being alive:

> Men do not sufficiently realise that their future is in their own hands. Theirs is the task of determining first of all whether they want to go on living or not. Theirs is the responsibility, then, for deciding if they want merely to live, or intend to make just the extra effort required for fulfilling, even on their refractory planet, the essential function of the universe, which is a machine for the making of gods. (1932: 54)

This chapter emphasizes creativity in relation to activist *practice* as an important counterpoint to the inappropriate perspective that technologies make revolutions possible. Practice theory, influenced by the writings of social theorists such as Pierre Bourdieu (1977), Sherry Ortner (1978), and Anthony Giddens (1994), discusses how individual or collective actions impact social or political structures of power. We describe a number of creative actions that activists have taken worldwide to contest injustice, and focus on these creative practices in relation to media and technology to recognize that these tools, like any others, can be shaped to support a range of causes.

Technologies can thus be viewed as part of the process of "place-making," which examines how a tool is used in relation to places, times, practices, and peoples (Massey 2005). We wish to humanize activism and creativity rather than naïvely deify technologies. Media technologies have always been part of assemblages shaped and produced by activists. This is true whether we speak of the role of the video of Rodney King's beating in relation to the Los Angeles riots or print within the French Revolution. And today it is true with respect to the internet.

Social Media Binaries

Clay Shirky's piece "The Political Power of Social Media" graced the cover of the influential *Foreign Affairs* magazine in November 2011. Influential in United States diplomatic circles, his article argues for the synergy between networked technologies and mass protests. Its position is consistent with Shirky's famous statement that "when we change the way we communicate we change society" (2008:17), presuming that on its surface the mere use of the internet supports democracy.

Shirky's position is consistent with the findings of scholars such as Philip Howard, whose research team identified heightened online activity before the full break-out of the Arab Spring. Howard and colleagues have argued that social media were utilized to share information about on-the-ground activity within the Arab world (Howard 2010; Howard & Hussain 2013). This is consistent with Zeynep Tufekci's argument that for activists there exists a collective action "'problem" that may be overcome through the use of social media:

> The "how" of social organizing matters because the means of connectivity impact the nature of a movement, the chance for its success, the tactics it can adopt – which in turn, impact its character –, the roles it can play, and the measures the state can deploy against it. All of these shape the nature, outlook, and the reach of the movement. (Tufekci 2011)

The position that online activity correlates with early (or prior) stages of protest is unsurprising, as it makes sense that internet-connected activists would use these media to spread their perspectives, and gather support. Such a position is described in research around "citizen journalism," namely the use of technology and the blogosphere to facilitate revolutionary conversation during times of political turmoil (Al-Rawi 2014). Seungahn Nah and Deborah Chung (2016), for example, have discussed how citizen journalism can work as a substitute for censored mainstream journalism in such periods of upheaval.

We recognize and respect such work. Indeed, it is unsurprising that online activity may circulate stories from the ground. Yet ending our analysis at this point would fail to consider the experiences of the majority of a population that may be technologically disconnected, as well as the other means by which they may protest or share information.

Revolutions and networks have existed long before Facebook or Twitter, and many have shaped the course of history as we know it. Moreover, the collective action problems of the past were clearly overcome in these cases. Indeed, technological connectivity may work against physical mobilization, particularly when it influences citizens to stay at home or more passively protest by merely remaining online. This is consistent with the position of Navid Hassanpour (2011), who points out that mobile phone and internet use was negatively correlated with physical protest during the Egyptian revolution. Yet when the Mubarak regime made the mistake of shutting down mobile phone and internet connectivity, it may have contributed to the spectacle of January 28, 2011, the largest day of protest.

Like the somewhat optimistic work we have presented, we note the work of several writers who presume that technologies may be incidental or even irrelevant in shaping political activism. For example, Evgeny Morozov (2011) has shared examples that demonstrate how regimes can subvert oppositional activity through using the internet. Consistent with this, Malcolm Gladwell, in his piece "Small Change: Why the Revolution Will Not be Tweeted" (2012), argues that social media technologies are useful for forming "weak ties," which assist the spreading of information during revolutions, yet fail to form "strong ties," which are needed to shape trust and leadership in a political movement.

Other writers, such as Nicholas Carr and Andrew Keen, have also weighed in with their doubts. Carr (2010) has argued that internet activity blocks one's ability to focus, process, and presumably reflect on information, which would seemingly stymie the capacity to protest effectively. Keen (2007), in turn, over-essentializes the internet to assume that it is nothing but a vehicle for narcissism and therefore "anti-social."

We appreciate the optimistic and skeptical positions taken by these writers. Yet what we believe is missing across these points is a relational analysis of the internet and social media that considers how it is mediated by the values, practices, contexts, and creativity of activists and citizens. What is missing is the consideration of assemblages that bring technologies into conversations with other factors in shaping political activism.

Participatory Politics

A positive step forward could be to think about the different manners by which internet use may shape "participation," or the engagement in political activism. With this approach, we can think about different types of participation and their implications. Our discussion of participation draws on the writings of media scholar Henry Jenkins, and considers the dimensions of "participatory politics."

A number of scholars, including this book's authors, had an online conversation on this topic in 2014, eventually published as a journal article (Couldry & Jenkins 2014). Within our discussion of participatory politics, Mirko Tobias Schaefer pointed out the distinction between explicit and implicit participation. *Implicit participation*, he argued, represents a mirage of civic engagement which in actuality may reinforce various structures of power. One's participation, from this perspective, just makes the rich richer. It assists advertising giants, technology corporations, and surveillance practices. This type of participation is myopic, personal, and occasionally self-indulgent. In contrast, Schafer claims that *explicit participation* reconceives digital platforms as allies in shaping a social or political cause. It is intentional appropriation in action.

Nico Carpentier and Natalie Fenton added to the conversation by observing that any discussion of participation must consider inequalities outside of the world of technology. No use of technology is in itself sufficient to overcome the structural and systemic inequalities that shape the "digital revolution". One can see this in the case of China, as noted by Jack Qiu, where passive participation around the internet is rampant without affecting political inequality. Qiu pointed out that the use of the Weibo social media platform by labor activists was insufficient to defend themselves from an attack by the state against their movement.

We thus note the importance of analyzing new technologies within a context of other networks and practices of political participation. It is a reminder that we must neither privilege nor dismiss technology in a reactionary way but instead learn from the peoples, places, contexts, and environments that shape assemblages of activism.

A Contextual Turn

Our goal is to understand how technologies like Facebook and YouTube are included within assemblages by activists who may use such tools. Rather than present a dismissive conclusion which presumes that technology use turns one into a "slacktivist" rather than an engaged activist, we can instead think more contextually, from the ground up.

It is important to note that infrastructures and systems build upon one another. Thus, we must not make the mistake of over-privileging the social networks shaped by new technology while forgetting that social networks are formed and sustained in many non-digital ways. Assemblages of activism may work across these networks to shape new formations. Politically subversive networks may be created and sustained by different groups of activists over many years.

For example, in Egypt, oppositional political networks have existed for decades. The spectacle of Tahrir Square must thus be seen relative to histories associated with the Muslim Brotherhood, which had existed as an underground oppositional organization across rural Egypt since 1912 (Al-Anani 2008). Another important example from Egypt that shaped the revolution is its robust labor movement, which dates back dozens of years. In the case of neighboring Tunisia, it is easy to conclude that Mohamed Bouazizi's act of self-immolation in December 2010 gave rise to a "YouTube revolution." Yet such a presumption fails to recognize that Bouazizi had strong connections to an oppositional labor movement for many years before his act of martyrdom seemingly ignited the Arab Spring.

Similarly, as Cesar Guzman-Concha notes in his analysis of the 2011 Chilean student movement, the movement "did not appear from nowhere. It built upon an organizational network students created for many years... within the boundaries of a well-known repertoire of conflict" (2012: 414). Gonzales further supports this conclusion, noting that "it is often the broader political climate that mobilizes [them] to action" (2008: 230). Thus, we see how networks brokered by "formal student organizations" were critical to the early days of this student movement (García, von Bülow, Ledezma, & Chauveau 2014).

Consistent with this, in the case of the Occupy movement, which eventually took on a transnational form, analysis shows that the original New York City-based Wall Street encampment can be traced to long-standing actions and campaigns led by housing activists from the Bronx. W. Lance Bennett and Alexandra Segerberg (2012) point out how the micro-operations of Twitter use during Occupy connected different networks in a meaningful yet loosely knit manner. The authors argue that one must consider the role of formal organizations in shaping collective action, differentiating between "crowd-enabled networks," where organization is nearly completely decentralized, such as in the case of flash mobs, and "organizationally enabled and brokered networks", where existing organizations play a larger role in shaping online and offline activity.

It is remarkable how far and wide the video of Bouazizi's immolation in Tunisia has spread, or that of the killing of Neda Aghan-Soltan in 2009 in the midst of Iran's Green Revolution; or how extensively the video of Freddie Gray's assault in Baltimore, captured on mobile phone in 2015, has influenced protests in the United States (Rentz 2015) and shaped popular awareness of the #BlackLivesMatter movement.

Consistent with this, Indignado protesters in Spain recognized the role of technologies to shape connections between themselves and the wider population (Rainsford 2011). Social media groups that initially formed online in Spain evolved into offline collectives that reorganized themselves without the use of these tools. Noting the problems with a surveillance-friendly Skype, new technologies such as Mumble were identified by activists to connect multiple encampments through real-time communications. The "Toque a bankia" Indignado campaign successfully incorporated a range of older and newer media technologies and tactics to shape the perception of the movement among various audiences both within Spain and worldwide. From its strategic use of hashtags to its use of a website to direct protesters to block various bank entrances across the nation, Toque a bankia revealed the power of working across media platforms to move past the limitations of each in shaping activism.

Additionally, within the Occupy movement, which, like the Chilean and Indignado case, was primarily based in parts of the world where internet access was more widespread, digital technologies helped connect occupations across the world using tools such as Live Stream (Costanza-Chock 2012). Occupiers recognized the potential of using Skype in connecting with and supporting those who had their bodies already in physical and public spaces. The famous "mic check" technique used at occupations, where messages would be repeated by groups of people so that everyone could hear, began to integrate the use of Skype, where voices would first be vocalized online, often from other Occupy encampments, and then be remediated via the "People's Mic" (Costanza-Chock 2012). This coordination between the mediation of voice and Skype, and technologies *between* physical encampments, is another example of how activists can reassemble tools and technologies to support their movements.

Thus, instead of simply assuming that in online actions lie a panacea for all offline protests, or of mistakenly assuming the opposite of this, scholars who look at information, networks, and social movements must consider the multiple stages, contexts, and factors that shape activism. Jennifer Earl and Katrina Kimport (2011), for example, argue that we can view the role of technology in three different ways: *e-movements*, which limit action to the online world; *e-mobilization*, where online activity directly facilitates offline actions; and *e-tactics*, which include both online and offline components that in their best moments are effectively coordinated.

Assembling and Disassembling

The examples we share across this chapter reveal that activist assemblages involving technology are neither inherently smooth, nor do they always translate into sustained effective political movements. Oppositional networks do not always come together to make revolutions possible, nor do historical movements necessarily give rise to newer inflections. Thinking about this relative to the case of social media raises interesting questions that encourage us to look at bridges between different forms of mediation. We can think about questions such as the following. How do Facebook groups shape existing activist networks? How may either of these shape international or domestic journalism, which in turn may influence those disconnected from internet technologies? How may hitting the "kill switch" on internet access shape other forms of network formation and activism? How are the invisible filters encoded into the recommendation and search algorithms within Facebook or Google connecting particular technology users with or disconnecting them from others? And how can online petitions shape offline strategies?

Paolo Gerbaudo argues that we must consider the "why" and "who" of protest without reducing a movement to a specific technology or networked system, such as the internet. Gerbaudo's book *Tweets and the Streets* (2012) argues for the importance of "choreography of assembly" and "choreographic leadership" to describe the mediation between technological and physical space, including online and offline worlds.

Like Gerbaudo, we work with the concept of assemblage across this book's chapters as a means of doing away with the myth of the internet as immaterial or fixed, instead arguing that it is not only socially and culturally constructed but also inclusive of personal, material, social, environmental, and institutional elements,.

The second half of this chapter considers many of these themes by telling the story and struggles of Mosireen, a Cairo-based activist collective dedicated to serving as the "media wing" of the Egyptian revolution. The collective's actions reveal the power of thinking past the limits of any singular technological assemblage to instead embrace the fluidity of improvisation, organization, and networking. This section will build on ethnography conducted in Egypt between 2011 and 2014 in revolutionary Cairo (Srinivasan 2010, 2013, 2014).

Intuition and Media Activism: Stories from the Mosireen Collective

We tried to think about how we were using technology and when it was useful and when it was not...we would not have gotten by without technology, but again [activism] dissolves back down to politics. Whether we would have won or lost – it would have happened on political terms and not technological terms.

(Sherief Gaber, April 2015)

These words, stated by activist Sherief Gaber, speak to an approach taken by the Mosireen collective that viewed the internet as one tool or platform amongst many in shaping the principles of the Egyptian revolution. With the goal of exceeding the boundaries of the computer, street, or any other single

Figure 3.2   The Tweet-Nadwa (or "Tweet up") bringing activists together with real-time conversations online in Cairo, June 2011
Source: Ramesh Srinivasan

form of mediation, Mosireen was born out of the unstable political environment of the 2011 Egyptian revolution. As a group of mostly artists and filmmakers, Mosireen recognized its expertise in creating, curating, remixing, and distributing media in support of the revolution. Yet the activism of most came out of an intuitive response to the events of January 2011, out of the need to "document something, shoot something, make something out of what we saw and could not believe... it was just an explosion of expression" (Salma Shamel, April 2015).

In this sense, the majority of collective members with whom we spoke saw themselves first and foremost as activists dedicated to the causes of "bread, freedom, and social justice" that served as the motto by protesters during the Egyptian uprising. They note in conversations with us that each of these causes speak to different facets of the Egyptian population and that to support them they would have to create, document, and share media that were similarly inclusive.

Collective members described their expertise in working with media as a means of sharing content within and across demographic boundaries within the nation. Yet as they posted pieces online, they recognized the shortcomings of relying on an internet laden with protocols and political and economic interests far removed from their own concerns. In that sense, the internet was no panacea for activists relative to Egyptian state and private media.

> We recognized that while social media bubbles are a hegemonic assemblage so too are the worlds of mainstream media networks in Egypt.... We thought about how we could generate our own assemblages by working with both of these and whatever else we could get our hands on. (Sherief Gaber, April 2015)

Despite these concerns, Mosireen members also explained to us that as of 2011 the internet was the most open media space in an Egyptian environment where "old" television and newspaper platforms represented the interests of the state or private corporations. The internet was neither highly censored nor policed space. Activists considered different media and technology platforms as part of a larger distribution strategy with a sense neither of what success would look like nor of its feasibility.

Meeting in Tahrir Square in January and February 2011, activists who formed the collective were attacked by state security forces and noticed how occupiers of the square responded with the chant "Look at what the army is doing." They were concerned that their fellow Egyptians outside of the square would remain unaware of such brutality from the regime, and would continue to be manipulated by powerful state and corporate media narratives.

> We had no way of expanding outside of the moment and activity of our chants of "Look at what the army is doing to us."...Until we became a marriage between the needs we all shared to generate change, to re-envision and provide tools of re-imagining our nation. We all met as filmmakers, activists, and individuals working within digital communities as bloggers and hackers. Yet importantly, we also convened together in-person, in [Tahrir] square. (Khalid Abdalla, May 2015)

Mosireen members recognized that their contributions lay in shaping the imagination of their fellow Egyptians in defending the objectives of their revolution. To do such, they needed to develop a coherent identity and trust one another. They would also have to create a physical space to meet while recruiting others, and recognized that they could not fight for their revolutionary aims merely by remaining online. Members began to learn why certain media pieces they would create might resonate with their fellow citizens. The goal became to shift the ecology of what stories were told to what audiences. This could not be achieved solely through online information-sharing, but in relation to an assemblage of spaces, infrastructures, and a reliable "brand." Activists would need to "build on existing pulses" (Omar Hamilton, April 2015), and create and distribute content accordingly.

Mosireen found its home in a historic building space in downtown Cairo because it no longer was needed in another media project that involved collective founder Khalid Abdalla, a well-known British-Egyptian actor who has starred in multiple international films, including *The Kite Runner* (2007). Having a space provided Mosireen a visible identity, not just allowing it to serve as a public symbol of the revolution,

Figure 3.3   Mosireen space
Source: Khalid Abdalla, Mosireen

but also supporting in-person sharing of stories and tactics. Over time, a range of activist communities made Mosireen's space temporarily their home, including graffiti artists and the organizers of the largely successful "No to Military Trials" campaign.

It is interesting to see the desire to be publicly visible in Mosireen's actions, and how this directly contrasts with the arguments that support anonymity in online-only activism. Despite creating a great deal of online content, there was value for Mosireen members coming together in person, connecting with those who "could come upstairs [to our office] in the middle of clashes downstairs on the street" (Khalid Abdalla, May 2015). The creative actions taken by Mosireen members required being mindful and aware of the volatile climate within Cairo and around the nation. The collective's goal was to activate their fellow citizens at catalytic moments, developing assemblages that juxtaposed technological and non-technological components to keep the revolution alive.

A critical moment for Mosireen arose with the Maspero massacre of October 9, 2011, less than nine months after the initial 18 days of revolution, which began on January 25, 2011. The massacre occurred via an attack by state security forces on protesters from Egypt's Coptic Christian minority. It was spun by the state media (via television and radio) as an attack by Christians on the army and by the international media as Muslim-on-Christian violence. Islamophobia was a sentiment that the military regime had long exploited under the ruse of maintaining security against "extreme elements" within Egypt. It also emboldened the military regime to maintain its long-standing assault on Egypt's 10 percent Christian minority.

Amidst the frenzy of Maspero, Mosireen members saw an opportunity to intervene by using low-cost video-capture and editing technology to "rip" content from state and corporate media networks and remix it with footage that they had physically shot. They focused on a clip they captured of a soldier shooting a civilian in the back.

The Maspero massacre was thus retold in a video produced by Mosireen that slowed down the frame rate of the footage of this brutal killing. Collective media makers edited this video by highlighting the soldier's gun with a red circle. Quickly posting this new piece on YouTube, the clip was viewed over 100,000 times on the night it was uploaded.

The example we share here from Maspero reveals intuition and creativity in action, where Mosireen members recognized their need to act in the moment, while also working to manipulate, appropriate, and remix content produced by their adversaries in the state and corporate media. By taking fragments from different television networks and their own footage to create a new assemblage, Mosireen could tell an authentic story of bravery and brutality that could influence the public's imagination. With this in mind, collective members Salma Shamel and Danya Nadar spoke with us about the power of manipulating images, drawing on tools and techniques from the history of cinema, citing examples from Russian montage and German propaganda films. These cinematic techniques could hold power in shaping the visceral, psychological, and emotional experiences of those who viewed Mosireen-produced content.

Mosireen's goal became to confront Egyptians with images, videos, and narratives they had not seen. They distributed content they believed to be authentic to the causes and voices behind the revolution yet painfully absent in mainstream media. Collective leaders saw that to do so they would need to construct an alternative media network and collaborate with various journalists, even those who worked for organizations who had misrepresented the revolutionary cause. They could not simply trust the internet "as is," nor could they trust existing Egyptian media networks. They would have to "reassemble" a network of online and offline connections to fight for their cause. This would require overcoming technological and demographic bubbles.

Overcoming Bubbles

> We all saw how different the world was outside of our computers, whether we were in a cab or on the street.... We realized that extending access to the internet just extended complacency, and that there is a shallowness to technology.
>
> (Omar Hamilton, April 2015)

As activist Omar Hamilton points out, Mosireen collective members were aware of the limitations of simply spreading the content they produced via the internet. Despite their use of YouTube to post videos, Twitter to engage with international journalists, and Facebook groups to share images and information, they recognized the shortcomings of these media. They thus strategically reassembled a system of information generation and propagation that connected the "street" and the "online network."

Sherief Gaber described to us how collective members viewed social media as the "mirror of Narcissus," citing Richard Sennett's important text *The Fall of Public Man* (1977). Sennett's argument is that the modernist legacies of the Enlightenment have transformed public consciousness into selfish myopia. Gaber explained that one could view our social media "filter bubbles" and their associated opaque algorithms accordingly.

This, however, did not mean that the internet was meaningless for collective members; instead it was but part of an assemblage of grassroots activism. We note that several Mosireen members described the internet as a "circuit," a dual-purpose metaphor that refers not only to electronic hardware but also to a self-referential closed space. Collective members recognized that they would have to create content that was captivating, digestible, and "modular" in its focus on specific subjects and topics. They would also need to devise mechanisms of distributing content to overcome the "closed circuit" of the Egyptian social media audience, which was demographically homogeneous and already likely splintered by filters and personalization algorithms. One means of overcoming this could be to create and project revolutionary stories into public spaces across the nation. So came the birth of Tahrir Cinema.

Tahrir Cinema became a conduit for the Mosireen collective to distribute its stories to offline audiences in the square that had marked the birth of Egypt's revolution. Tahrir Cinema also represented an assemblage in which digital technologies collided with bed sheets, projectors, cement, tents, bodies, and chairs. The effort shifted revolutionary narratives out of siloed online environments and into collective spaces of viewing. The cinema screenings included pieces from a media archive that Mosireen had been assembling since February 2011.

Figure 3.4   Tahrir Cinema
Source: Sherief Gaber, Mosireen

The story of Tahrir Cinema reveals how activists can resist the filters and constraints of a single form of mediation to move *between and across* platforms. Mosireen's media practices shifted between video cameras, online environments, archives, and public spaces. They recognized that none of these are sufficient in isolation but all have something to contribute when viewed as part of an assemblage.

During the sit-in of July 8, 2011, a first screening occurred in the square where protesters had gathered intermittently since that January. Mosireen members recognized that they would have to carefully curate the videos they showed, and that their collective viewing could activate their fellow citizens in the square.

> The footage we showed that night was no longer stuck online or on our cameras. The voices taken away from every person in Egypt could be brought back to them through these screenings. It was extraordinary to see the audience come to us, ask questions about screenings, borrow USB sticks to copy content from us, start clapping and performing with the footage they would see. (Khalid Abdalla, May 2015)

Nina Mollerup and collective member Sherief Gaber (2015) have recently co-authored a paper reflecting on the street screenings of Tahrir Cinema. Discussing Tim Ingold's discussion of knowledge as situated, embodied, and interactional (2007), they argue that the collective viewing of the screenings speaks to the importance of *knowing with* rather than *knowing from* the videos that were shown. The interactivity between people, the screen, time periods, and places in which the screenings occurred cannot be reduced simply to the media object or platform itself. Screenings were as different as they were similar, contingent on the political climate, time, place, and content. No media piece could be understood without seeing it as an assemblage that also featured people, places, and environments.

Mosireen members explained their vision that Tahrir Cinema could "go viral." Not only did they hope for the media they screened to travel far and wide, but they hoped that what could emerge were multiple Mosireen collectives, only loosely tied to their original Cairo origins. Shifting away from the single place of Tahrir square or city of Cairo to multiple streets and regions around the nation became a strategy around the same time as Tahrir Cinema began to take hold. Using connections with various political organizations, such as the Revolutionary Youth coalition, media activism workshops were co-organized by Mosireen in the Sinai region and in Aswan, one of the largest cities in southern Egypt. The workshops focused on citizen journalism, including training participants to use their mobile phones to document and share their experiences in the midst of the changing political landscape. The goal was for Mosireen to rhizomatically mutate into multiple forms in many locations, decentralized from Cairo and reconstituted within working-class and rural communities nationwide. Members hoped that as the concept of Mosireen traveled it would take on a local life of its own, reassembled in relation to people, objects, places, and practices that were most meaningful to support the revolution across the nation.

Khalid Abdalla explained to us that Mosireen's "loose infrastructure" allowed it to function as a network, adapting to varying contexts and defying the formal structure of institutions that hold defined leadership roles, governance practices, and hierarchies. This is consistent with the culture of the collective, where members are empowered to act autonomously, and only loosely needing to follow the actions of one another. Mosireen's lack of history and its general mission of "serving the revolution" gave it the space to dynamically adapt, "shifting our meanings, identities, and strategies as we went along, with the simple goal of lighting as many wildfires as possible" (Khalid Abdalla, May 2015).

That said, while in many ways Mosireen was able to escape the barriers of hierarchy and centralization, it must also be seen as *situated*, in relation to particular places, people, and activities. How, then, could it successfully reach larger numbers in a country of 85 million?

Viral Media

"There was no shortage of footage, but it wasn't reaching people," says Sally Toma (2015), "We had to bring the revolution back to the people." When online dissemination also proved not to be effective enough to change public opinion, in the spirit of Tahrir Cinema the idea was hatched to reach people by utilizing public space as a medium of political expression and information dissemination.

The street screenings of the Aaskar Kazeboon project further decentralized the activities of Mosireen to transform any community or square in Egypt into a hub for media activism. It took the specificity of Tahrir Cinema while providing for the opportunity for it to recombine itself across the nation. In doing so, Kazeboon, like Tahrir Cinema, reassembled digital narratives alongside non-digital components to empower the Egyptian activist imagination.

Kazeboon, Arabic for "The Military are Liars," countered the stories of the military by asking citizens to share videos that captured the lies of the regime and screen these in their own communities (Eskander 2013). Initially devised by friends of the Mosireen collective, the effort helped produce a viral and decentralized set of counter-narratives to those of the military regime (Abaza 2013; Khamis, Gold & Vaughn 2012) and later to the Muslim Brotherhood presidency. Like Tahrir

Cinema, Kazeboon became a mechanism of empowering people without internet or social media access to create and share their stories and experiences (Austin-Holmes forthcoming).

It is important to note that like Tahrir Cinema, Kazeboon functions without the need for any connective infrastructure, instead only requiring bed sheets, the rental of a projector, and a device that can capture image or video, such as a low-cost mobile phone. It is an assemblage that can take on the qualities of a decentralized network without relying on any internet technology. It resembles an internet without any wires or connective infrastructure.

Organizers of the idea explained to us that they had no control over how far the initiative would spread. Rumors are that there were over 600 screenings in the nation at its peak in July 2012, and in at least eight countries abroad. Over 10,000 volunteers supposedly screened videos in every governorate within Egypt. The unhinging of this campaign from Cairo allowed it to spread far and wide. By covering topics such as the absence of food, healthcare, and housing, the circulated videos began to speak to the local concerns shared by a far wider range of citizens who could create and share videos within their communities based on the concerns they held.

It is important to point out that both the Kazeboon and Mosireen actions are challenged by the factors that make them potent: their abilities to scale. Offline revolutionary activities supported by each were often restricted to specific places and times. While these particularities represent in part the strength of an activist assemblage, they suffer from the absence of scalability, searchability, persistence, and other affordances that characterize the internet and social media platforms in their best moments. The internet is a decentralized network, but it is also at times easy to bring nodes of this network into conversation with one another.

Where Assemblages Cannot Tread

The Kazeboon campaign was at its height of popularity during the worst public moments of the governing regimes, whether in late 2011, when the economy was suffering, or in much of 2012, when the Muslim Brotherhood regime had made a number of significant economic and political miscalculations.

It was in these moments that the creative and improvisatory media practices of Mosireen and Kazeboon were most successful. Their exploits of disassembly used overlapping networks of technology, community, and urban infrastructure. At these times, they were able to tap into counter-narratives that were easy to find given the unpopularity of the state. These counter-narratives brought together the causes of the revolution ("bread, freedom, and social justice") to shape popular mobilization and political consciousness.

Yet, due to their grassroots basis, on their own such campaigns could not transform a traumatized political and economic environment, much less confront the "deep state" (Moyers 2014) that has controlled Egyptian institutional, economic, and political resources for decades. Revolutions, present and past, often produce political institutions to respond to the concerns raised through these activist movements. Yet if these causes became fodder for creative manipulation, a schism could be constructed that could fragment precarious activist coalitions.

This is best illustrated in the unfortunate events starting at the end of June 2013 in the midst of the Tamarod activist campaign (which only peripherally involved Mosireen), which also maintained online and offline components. Tamarod, the Arabic word for "Rebel," was initiated as an online petition at the moment when the Muslim Brotherhood regime, which had cut a deal with the "deep state" military, was least popular. The movement quickly shifted offline as activists recognized that signing paper petitions and letting photocopiers do their work could reach far more in Egypt than a webpage, tweet, or Facebook group. Activists estimated that over 25 million Egyptians signed the Tamarod petition asking for then President Morsi to step down. Yet as protests erupted to challenge the legitimacy of one unfair regime, another quickly emerged to cement its power. The military regime, which continued to control many aspects of Egypt even with the success of the Muslim Brotherhood in elections, exploited the protests in a coup to topple the government, and imprison and kill numerous activists.

Standing in Tahrir Square with hundreds of thousands of other Egyptians in the days after June 30, 2013, Mosireen members have explained to us that they noticed one significant difference compared to their protest activities in January 2011. This was the appearance of a military helicopter above their heads. Instead of attacking the protesters, however, the helicopter dropped Egyptian flags on them (figure 3.5), symbolically articulating the military's kinship with the Tamarod movement. And as this happened, activists recognized that their causes had been stolen from them, and their revolutionary energies had been co-opted by the face of the deep state.

Subverting the protests through these symbolic acts, the military took power via coup in the days that followed, claiming allegiance with the Egyptian protesters, and deposing the Muslim Brotherhood regime. All of a sudden the gas shortages that drove so many protesters into the streets and squares of Egypt went away and the inflated prices of food dropped to more acceptable levels. For many in Egypt these events seemed incredible, reaffirming what was once a blind faith in the military before 2011. Unfortunately most within the nation either failed to see the ruse or had grown weary

Figure 3.5 Military helicopter dropping flags on protesters in Cairo's Tahrir Square, early July 2013
Source: Ramesh Srinivasan

of the instability that came after a revolution that was just three years old.

The military regime's control of capital, industry, and land across Egypt meant it could manipulate factors that shaped discontent. Although activists derisively referred to the "Macaroni Military," owing to its ownership of macaroni factories, most working-class Egyptians still embraced the retaking of power by the armed forces as they knew that this might bring about economic "stability." Tapping into the reserves of money and commodities it controlled, the military complemented the symbolic intervention of dropping Egyptian flags on protesters by funding a series of manipulative subsidies to temporarily transform the economic climate and shape public opinion. Mosireen was in trouble.

> We got stuck in a position where our videos no longer mattered, our street actions would mean our death, and no one cared about our workshops any longer....What do we do? We can't just keep posting videos that no one cares about, that no one watches. We are now back [to] where we were, stuck in the middle of the circuit. But today no one cares. (Sherief Gaber, April 2015)

Sherief Gaber's words illustrate the crisis that faced Mosireen in July 2013 and in the years since. While the collective's activities were unhinged from the existing limitations of social media and internet platforms, they no longer had a clear mechanism by which they could organize or a set of principles that they could follow that could help sustain their movement with fellow Egyptians. They had lost their control over the narrative of the revolution.

This partially describes Egypt into the early months of 2017. Many members of the Mosireen collective have told us of the depression they have felt in the years since July 2013, and others have shared their bewilderment as their fellow Egyptians re-embrace an oppressive military that has strangled democracy and social justice for decades.

> We are now stuck in the games of popular culture, stuck in spaces of slacktivism, where clicking poses as acting. We're stuck trying to make more captivating videos online in a world where no one sees these. The time will come where we are

able to stand up yet again to the limiting discourses of social media. (Sherief Gaber, April 2016)

Despite the creativity and potency of the assemblages they produced in 2011 and after, Mosireen members recognize that today they must return to the traditional internet where in many ways they were most familiar, an environment where they can vent, comment, and reflect. Yet, as we have described, these environments and their filters make them hardly "social."

At its peak, Mosireen-produced content was popular online, but as we have explained throughout this chapter, this had little to do solely with the online world. Mosireen's popularity on YouTube had a great deal to do with the climate on the street and the connections made with other spaces and actors. Yet no matter how many creative tactics one may use, to permanently overthrow an institution of power, the basis of its power must be overcome.

Activist Assemblages Onward

This chapter has taken aim at a myth of the internet as a singular, unified space that fuels democracy and grassroots activism. Our goal was not to dismiss the existence and potential meaning of digitally networked platforms but to anchor our understanding of these relative to how they are accessed, by whom, and with what filters and constraints. Situating technologies within this complex matrix of factors may not give rise to easy buzzwords such as "Net Delusion," "Small Change," or "Here Comes Everybody," but it does allow us to learn from powerful stories of political and social struggle in today's world.

Mosireen activists have expressed a range of sentiments about how they have evolved since their movement was halted in 2013. Some have gone back to the drawing board, thinking about a way to develop and deploy technologies that would be more internally aligned with the activities of future social movements. These individuals have recognized that merely making more videos is not sufficient at this time, as the content they create can easily be used to subvert rather than support their political intentions. Other collective members have gone back to work in the creative and artistic industries. Some have resolved to not think too much about the sad political turn Egypt has taken, where activists have been jailed and tortured and Muslim Brotherhood members have been assassinated.

Mosireen members have shared with us their continued goal of keeping the history of the revolution alive via the digital archive they have assembled. Their goal is not to be an "instant nostalgia machine for a very depressed Egypt" (Sherief Gaber, April 2015) but eventually to be part of an evolving future. There is a belief amongst some collective members that there will be a time when activist networks and practices will be reassembled in new forms, but when that time is and what this new assemblage will look like remain unclear. Despite the spectacular events of January 2011, activists recognize that the impacts of their actions may not be always measurable nor result in short-term change. Instead of seeing this as reason for resignation, there may be great power in respecting and affirming the sadness they feel. Depression is often seen as a pathology to be rid of, rather than an emotional, psychological, and material state to inhabit and be mindful of.

Our goal has been neither to deify nor to exoticize the example of Mosireen but to ask readers to think about what we can learn from their story. Khalid Abdalla has expressed his belief that the Egyptian narrative of revolution will continue to unfold. Citing Jean-Luc Godard's *Notre Musique* (2004), Abdalla has explained to us his hope that Egypt will now enter a moment of fiction, of "long-form narrative," where its current depression can give rise to a new imaginary. Activists may find a perspective, through fiction and narrative, of a new "horizon" that defies existing ideological constraints.

A revolution, for Abdalla and others within Mosireen, is better understood as a process rather than a specific outcome or state. The process is one of "radical becoming" rather than "radical actualization." Radical becoming, in the spirit of assemblage theory, represents a "horizon" that respects and embraces complexity and difference. Explicitly discussing Deleuze's seminal *Difference and Repetition* (1994), Abdalla explained that in today's Egypt there is a myth that activist causes will be perpetually oppressed. Mosireen and others must do away with this form of thinking and instead embrace indeterminacy to allow the "splinters" of their causes to give way to new formations. Patchwork constructs such as creating new political parties in today's Egypt may do little to cultivate a new imagination that will challenge and overcome the military regime down the line. Abdalla concludes:

> Building a political party during a revolution is equivalent to building a house during an earthquake. A revolutionary period is confused as radical actualization but I believe it is a period of radical becoming. Over time our cause will evolve and ultimately overcome the organs of the deep state. (Khalid Abdalla, May 2015)

In the same spirit, Mosireen and future activist collectives across the world can continue to embrace a creative optimism that resists the dualism of "success"/"failure" dialectics. Deleuze stated that "I make, remake and unmake my concepts along a moving horizon, from an always decentered center, from a displaced periphery which repeats and differentiates them" (1994: xx–xxi). We note that what Deleuze (and Abdalla) ask for here is an affirmation of undecidability amongst activists. This story rings true within Egypt and other parts of the world that have witnessed recent social and political movements.

Activists in Egypt can embrace the long form, continuing to intuitively and creatively view their nation to imagine new futures. Mosireen members' epiphanic moments came about when they shifted away from a pre-set plan, fixed identity, or any attached form of mediation and trusted their improvised and creative abilities to act upon their environment. They recognized the shortcomings of the assemblage of the internet as it stood and moved past this by working across technologies, peoples, and places to fight for a democratic Egypt. A new space was opened up when Mosireen, like other activist groups we have described in this chapter, resisted the manufactured identities produced by mainstream media that described its members as a "Facebook generation" or failed revolutionaries. Deleuze has argued that when life appears standardized and stereotyped, it is all the more important to inject art and imagination into its habitual processes, to become "the poet, who speaks in the name of a creative power, capable of overturning all orders and representations in order to affirm difference" (1968: 53).

The examples we have shared in this chapter encourage us to disengage from an attachment to specific platforms, tools, or modes of mediation. They ask us to think "after the internet" to see activism that includes and builds upon existing technologies and infrastructures. Just as it is shortsighted to view the effects of a movement simply by looking at the short-term changes it effects, it is also incomplete to limit one's understanding of that movement by looking at a single point or mode of mediation. The value of thinking across multiple assemblages is in how it empowers an understanding of the creative and intuitive ways by which activists fight for social change. This, we believe, is what Deleuze speaks about when he asks us to take a poetic turn in our thinking of voice and power, in resisting the constraints of habituation to affirm difference. Just as we cannot or should not homogenize the distinctive movements from Chile, Spain, Occupy, and Egypt, we must not judge the success or failure of a revolution based on the misnomer of "Facebook Revolution." As Wael Eskandar, an ally of Mosireen and organizer of Kazeboon, wrote to the authors:

> But just so that I'm not talking about a dream that may never come true, there's value in enduring nevertheless, and even if we are all to vanish, we should not vanish without a fight. And just so we're clear, it's not about going out to protest and fight a losing battle, it's about the battle within you...do not let your ideas and ideals vanish without a fight. (Wael Eskandar, June 2015)

The causes of social, economic, and environmental justice so admirably pursued by activists in our world most likely will continue to involve the internet and digital networks as part of an assemblage, yet never in isolation. As we reflect on the relationships between the internet and activism, we must think "after the (existing) internet" and instead learn from its potentially powerful relationship with institutions, places, and peoples.

4
After the Cloud: Do Silk Roads Lead to Data Havens?

This book has described assemblages "after the internet" that speak to grassroots voices of diverse global and indigenous communities, hacktivists, and revolutionaries and protesters in Egypt and across the world. In this chapter we will discuss a central feature associated with the internet and digitally networked communications, that of *personal data*. The destiny of user data – where it is stored and how it is exploited is at the heart of struggles around what the internet is or may be.

As we described in this book's introduction, both metaphors and myths can obscure as much as they illuminate. The current metaphor that seems to be uncritically accepted to describe corporate and governmental practices around data is the *cloud* (but see counter-examples: Cubitt 2016; Holt & Vonderau 2015; Mosco 2014).

We must ask the question: where does data go when it goes into the "cloud"? The answer has increasingly become data centers, large corporate warehouses with computers, air conditioners, offices, and engineers. These centers are developed to store and process immense amounts of data. Described as the "nucleus of the digital universe" (Nasdaq 2013), data centers rent storage space to major companies, governments, and civil society actors to process the present-day "data deluge" (*The Economist* 2010). These centers require robust interconnectivity provided by fiber-optic cables that run through cities and the countryside, are underground and under the sea, and form the infrastructure that is the global internet. The geographies traversed by these internet cables are also jurisdictional, as national and extra-territorial laws regulate where data can flow. Thus instead of being falsely viewed as immaterial or deterritorialized, digital infrastructures need to be understood in relation to local communities, businesses, and landscapes.

This chapter considers both the problems and the potentials associated with the opaque routing of personal data to massive privatized data centers far away from the sight of the users from whom this is collected. Instead of simply taking these data infrastructures for granted, we consider how privacy-minded individuals, activists, and enterprises are attempting to reimagine what a data center could be, by focusing on attempts to create a *data haven* in Iceland that can serve as an example to be taken up in other parts of the world. A data haven is a place designed to be secure from surveillance or acquisition by third parties, including police forces.

This chapter focuses on the Icelandic data haven example because it represents an alternative imaginary of a cloud that is no longer singular and opaque but instead reterritorialized by placing the internet within an assemblage that includes *national policy, extra-legal attempts to capture and manipulate data*, and a *cultural vision of social liberalism*.

Like the other cases we describe throughout this book, these assemblages highlight points of contestation and risks to their viability. Indeed, our analysis concludes that a legally mandated safe harbor for data is not sufficient to overcome the crises faced today around data exploitation and surveillance. This is a sobering reminder that national legislation and policy can be threatened by other laws and surveillance technologies. Yet it also shows that we need not take the current opaque practices of capturing and manipulating data for granted, and that alternative assemblages can emerge.

Watching Clouds

Personal information is big business; the "new oil" of the digital economy. For example, Axciom is a massive data brokerage firm that is responsible for 12 percent of the $11 billion annual direct marketing industry. Closely analyzing the social media signals of billions of users, Axciom sells to the financial and healthcare industries access to specific demographics such as "potential inheritor," "adult with senior parent," and households with a "diabetic focus" (Singer 2013). Similarly, it may be surprising that the business model for Facebook, a company worth hundreds of billions of dollars with 1.5 billion monthly active users uploading more than 350 million photos a day, is no different. Money and power are increasingly acquired by soliciting, collecting, analyzing, and selling personal data.

While the management and monetization of data is central to information businesses, it is also integral to surveillance programs administered by the nation-state. The US National Security Agency (NSA) had a similarly ambitious approach to that of Facebook or Axciom, as revealed in its goals: "Sniff it all, know it all, collect it all, process it all, exploit it all, partner it all" (NSA 2014) (see figure 4.1). Its Utah-based Data Center (figure 4.2) cost $1.5 billion, is between 1 million and 1.5 million square feet in size, uses 1.7 million gallons

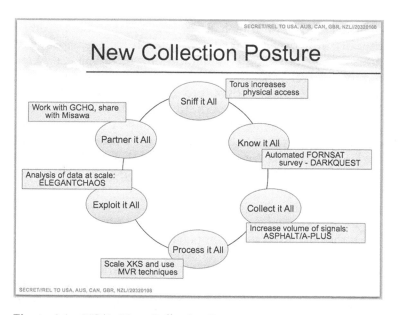

Figure 4.1 NSA's New Collection Posture
Source: Wikimedia Commons

Figure 4.2   NSA Data Center in Utah
Source: Wikimedia Commons

of water a day to cool hard drives, and has data storage capacity of between 3 and 12 exabytes. It has the capacity to process all forms of communication, including "parking receipts, travel itineraries, bookstore purchases, and other digital 'pocket litter'" (Bamford 2012; see also Hill 2013). With consumer drones overhead complete with 4K video cameras, GPS-tracking phone apps, prolific CCTV, and trash cans and refrigerators self-monitoring their users, perhaps we are living today in a "post-privacy world" (Levin 2015; Pagliery 2015; Spivack 2013).

Yet it is not just the data of citizens that may no longer be private but also that of corporations and governments. A bright red grinning skull greeted television producers at Sony when they accessed their computers on November 24, 2014. Sony had been "cracked," an action that included a hack of 47,000 Social Security numbers and embarrassing celebrity emails (Musil 2014). In another example, between August 18 and 20, 2015, the hacker group "Impact Team" released 80 gigabytes of data from the subscription-based pro-infidelity website Ashley Madison. In an interview, the hackers claimed:

"[I]t was easy. For a company whose main promise is secrecy, it's like you didn't even try, like you thought you had never pissed anyone off" (Cox 2015). The hacked database is searchable and includes 15,000 .gov, .mil, and other government accounts, fueling the sense that "[a]fter Ashley Madison surely nobody believes that privacy is an option any more" (Nicholson 2015).

Taken together, the 10 biggest breaches of supposedly secure data amount to the unauthorized release of almost a billion records (Palermo & Wagenseil 2015). Indeed, whether seen as a dystopian "Era of Surveillance" or a utopian "Age of Transparency," it seems impossible to not leave a personal trail online (Spivack 2013). We have become habituated to leaks, experiencing them as continuous spectacles. We have become numb to their velocity and sheer volume (Colvin 2017; Follis & Fish 2017). It is not simply the release of data that has become problematic for governments, corporations, or private citizens, it is the ways in which this data has been assembled by their adversaries, enabling surveillance and control, extra-judicial policing, the loss of money and resources, and the smearing of one's image.

A vigorous debate has begun in parliaments and boardrooms of major companies around the world instigated by controversies surrounding Edward Snowden, cybercriminals, whistle-blowers, and corporate espionage. This has centered on the issue of whether governments can or should attempt to control the flow of information. Activists have argued that how we preserve and transmit data impacts the privacy of our children, the preservation of healthy ecosystems, the robustness of our economics, the accountability of our politics, and our autonomy over our personal information. The current generation is unprecedented in the expectations it faces to be constantly visible in exchange for social services, and this trend may continue depending on the outcome of such debates.

Naturally, privacy is a shifting concept, manifesting itself differently over places and times (Altman, 1975; Marwick, Murgia-Diaz, & Palfrey 2010; Solove 2007). Nevertheless, however defined or historicized, mass unwarranted surveillance has made "virtual privacy" an oxymoron. While these issues disproportionately affect communities that are digitally connected, as the goal of connecting the "last billion" fueled by companies such as Facebook or Google pushes forward, it may only be a matter of years before the data of the entire planet's population is open for sale or surveillance.

Thus, important ethical questions must be asked. One of the foremost is whether we should accept the supposed benefits of personalization. For "total personalization, you have to be totally transparent," according to Kevin Kelly, founder of *Wired* and self-proclaimed techno-utopian (Stibel 2013). Kelly, like many others, treats the internet as autonomous and divine, as driven by its own reflexive push to "innovate." We must consider what Kelly means by transparency and to whom such transparent information is visible and beneficial. We can ask whether transparency is a state requested by technology users, or by those individuals or institutions that benefit from access to this data.

Big Data and the Metaphor of the Cloud

While it may bring to mind images of weightlessness, and therefore blank acceptance, the metaphor for data storage, the *cloud*, has a very weighty material existence. From one perspective, clouds appear otherworldly. They seem to be autonomous and natural. Yet Tung-hui Hu (2015) has persuasively argued that, consistent with earlier technologies, the technological and corporate implementation of the cloud has undermined democratic accountability while supporting systems of political inequality. The cloud is in fact an assemblage that is technologically and politically connected to other devices, data centers, institutions, and systems of power. Like drones and stratospheric balloons, the cloud exists mostly out of our view, allowing it to avoid scrutiny and interrogation. By taking stratospheric flight it exists beyond regulation and protest, capable of raining down connectivity without dealing with the messiness of user approval (Fish 2015).

This is all the more important because associated with the cloud is today's revolution in "big data." While this is lauded for its technical and democratic potential, we must scrutinize the production and profiteering systems associated with this metaphor. Some have argued that both the cloud and its engagement with big data have brought about a decrease in political freedom and personal autonomy and an increase in surveillance and informational consumerism (Lanier 2010; Morozov 2013).

The immateriality of the cloud and big data seems to remove our need to understand how these systems and infrastructures impact the world in which we live. For example, storing much of the world's information results in 2 percent of present annual carbon dioxide emissions. The ecological impact of data centers often directly contradicts the progressive or "green" claims of this industry (Cubitt, Hassan, & Volkmer 2011). A passive acceptance of the discourse of the cloud shapes how we frame data centers as sacrosanct private property rather than seeing them as a regulatable body or as transformable into the infrastructure for a digital commons. danah boyd and Kate Crawford describe the cultural mythologies of big data, or "the widespread belief that large data sets offer a higher form of intelligence and knowledge that can generate insights that were previously impossible, with the aura of truth, objectivity, and accuracy" (2012: 663).

There is a great deal of discussion today that evangelizes big data and its supposedly transformative influence on the agendas of scientists, corporations, and governments. Some scholars are worried that a methodological move toward big data will see science transition from an explanatory model based on causality to correlation to a much weaker explanatory framework. The claim is that big data will help to solve a range of problems, from disease to forest fire prediction (Mayer-Schönberger & Cukier 2013). Others celebrate that the explanatory power of big data means the end of interpretive social science as we know it (Anderson 2008). From this perspective, "big data" mythologizes the powers of data and marginalizes humanism (Couldry 2013).

Major debates exist in social science about how local events masquerade as evidence of global systems (Ong & Collier 2005). For example, the "variegations" of capitalism are offered as examples of its local adaptability; evidence of how capitalism develops to fit specific ecologies, trade patterns, and cultural beliefs (Jessop 2012). Far from creating uniformity, an engaged ethnographic perspective sees how the internet may facilitate local cultural values, ontologies, and vernaculars (Castells

2009; Miller & Slater 2000; Postill 2011). Scholars astutely have pointed out how locality – including geography, regulations, and local customs – affects not only diverse online communities but also the material infrastructure of the internet (Graham 2011). While many have discussed a monolithic "digital capitalism," fewer have developed empirical studies into the infrastructure that supports it and the diverse ways local communities have responded to that infrastructure (Schiller 2000; Suarez-Villa 2012). This book supports this growing body of grounded, ethically driven scholarship. This chapter in particular investigates how Icelandic politicians and activists attempt to mobilize their local jurisdictions to send reverberations of privacy centrifugally outward through the global internet assemblage.

Investigations into how the internet is localized can thus be linked to a scholarly agenda that documents the materiality of media. An emphasis on the material aspects of media production and dissemination has been a key debate in the history of media studies (McLuhan 1964; Kittler 1994; Postman 1993) and one receiving a due renaissance of late (Parks & Starosielski 2015). Recently scholars have focused on the materiality of media infrastructure, including the undersea cable infrastructure of the South Pacific (Starosielski 2015), data centers in the Pacific Northwest (Blum 2012), and telecommunications infrastructures in California (Parks 2013). Conceptual and analytic advances in media studies have identified the study of information infrastructure as an opportunity to witness how locations are integrated into the global information economy (Gillespie, Boczkowski, & Foot 2014). This approach encourages scholars to explore outside the "digital enclosure" (Andrejevic 2009) and combine intellectual labor with analysis of the "geophysical positions" of information infrastructure (Parks 2013: 18).

Despite such important research, few scholars have thought critically about how data centers accrue political and economic power through a domination of place (Sack 1983). Previous scholarship on data centers has focused on the United States, and investigated data centers as ecological dilemmas (Cubitt, Hassan, & Volkmer 2011; Hogan 2015), as media infrastructure (Holt & Vonderau 2015), or as systems of centralized power (Filippi & McCarthy 2012; Mosco 2014). This chapter contributes to these important studies by focusing on *territoriality*: the political powers linked to the control over place (Daskal 2015; Harvey 2001; Soja 1989). This research contributes to theorizing how geography and infrastructures are co-constituted (Barad 2003; Jasanoff 2004). One way of interpreting this is to focus on regulation and the growing powers of the informational state to assert its territoriality, providing evidence of how power can be articulated relative to space (Kitchin & Hubbard 1999; Sassen 2004). We focus on this issue through a story from Iceland.

Policy, the State, and Information Activism

In Iceland, information activists, some within the government and others who have volunteered for or collaborated with WikiLeaks, have come together under the organization the International Modern Media Institute (IMMI), since the financial crisis in 2008, to put forth a body of legislation that would make the country the most secure location in the world for the preservation of data. These laws include source protection from Sweden, communication protection from Belgium, freedom of information provisions from Norway and Estonia, libel protection from New York state, and other best practices from across the world (Babbage 2010).

While these measures have yet to become law, the Icelandic parliament has supported IMMI. If set into law, these proposals and several others would transform Iceland into the first prominent "safe harbor" data haven on the planet. Its emergence would have both political impacts on information activists and financial consequences for the digital industries in Iceland and throughout the world.

The IMMI example is one where laws, policies, and governmental practices have been cast into an assemblage with data centers and the internet to promote the values of anti-surveillance and personal freedom. Tatevik Sargsyan has discussed the process of changing government practices to bypass or rework laws and technologies through partnerships and negotiations with information intermediaries. He describes the ways in which these intermediaries transfer and store data "in geographically disproportionate data centers, allowing select governments to claim jurisdiction over the data and access them by imposing various surveillance laws" (Sargsyan 2016: 2223). Consistent with this, Mél Hogan (2013) calls for a reinvestment in understanding and considering the materiality of data, and what it means to be encouraged to think abstractly about the distant and/or inaccessible servers on which personal data is located.

We note one important case that exemplifies the difficulties of generating a data haven, the case of the Silk Road, a darknet bazaar discussed in some detail in chapter 2. The Silk Road server – containing a trove of incriminating information about the selling of drugs, arms, and other contraband – was housed by an Icelandic data center. In the course of a 2014 US FBI raid, the Silk Road server was confiscated from the Icelandic data center. While IMMI did not intend to protect the storage of data used in the retailing of contraband, the relative ease with which the FBI acquired this server shows some of the shortcomings of the data haven proposal. For instance, while the data center intermediary was not liable for the Silk Road data it stored, it was still left unable to defend against its acquisition by the FBI. The data center retained information about the Silk Road that it was forced to provide to the FBI for its investigation. What may be needed are more courageous leaders and a publicly financed data commons capable not only of withstanding hacking by international agencies such as the NSA, but also resisting the efforts of FBI agents.

The efforts to create a data haven via IMMI may thus be challenged by the forces of international criminal investigation. Yet IMMI is also interesting in at least two notable respects. First, its effort to use geopolitical sovereignty to engineer an internet of different laws and regulations can be seen as an attempt to fragment the internet, creating geographical balkanization (Goldsmith & Wu 2006). Insofar as the internet is viewed as the infrastructure to support the "free flow" of information, data haven cases represent an attempt to block this through assemblages which leverage geographical jurisdiction. Second, we note that such balkanization is designed to increase "freedom" of information and protect the efforts of transparency activists who "open" up governments and corporations. Thus, the paradox is that while the original effort of IMMI is to reorganize the exterior forces of the assembled internet into a balkanized zone of difference, the end goal is to reassemble a micro-zone of progressive liberty.

This point relates to the existence of different *intranets* in Iran, China, Cuba, and North Korea. Here one sees how different national laws shape digital communication networks based on distinct legal and infrastructural intermediaries. One rarely thinks about these examples relative to the developed countries of the North Atlantic as these intranets are often tied to legacies of authoritarianism and censorship. Yet it is interesting that IMMI's efforts would have a similar impact on the *structural* level of the internet, wherein data in Iceland would be subject to the specific laws and regulations of a small island. In the language of assemblage theory, efforts toward territoriality – that is, a form of localized power – would seek to leverage the chaotic heterogeneity of the internet. The locking down of an intranet specific to Iceland's geography is an example of infrastructural malleability and an attempt to rematerialize data practices and infrastructures (Furlong 2011).

We contrast this to the increasingly deterritorialized manner in which the internet is treated today. Here the constitutive component of geography plays a less impactful role. The territorialized space of travel and flow is striated, punctuated with the walls, caverns, and borders of the state, which complicate and confound the myth of the internet as singular or immaterial (DeLanda 2006). A smooth, or deterritorialized, space is one in which Iceland "goes with the flow" of global capital and the surveillance apparatus. In contrast, IMMI represents a territorialization of the internet, the production of a space of blockage.

IMMI is thus a reassembly of the exterior forces of law and technology, of jurisprudence and undersea cables. This confounds the myth that the internet's essential "nature" leads it toward the friction-free flow of capital, media, and data. Thus it is surprising that in the hands of the freedom-loving, socially liberal, and libertarian technologists of Iceland, we see the development of an internet of striation and territoriality.

Iceland as a Data Haven: The History of an Idea

What, then, are the most important factors that shaped IMMI? Our historical unpacking of this case starts with John Perry Barlow (see Introduction) giving a keynote speech on the evolution of communications at the Icelandic Digital Freedom Conference in July 2008. He discussed technological evolution from the origin of speech in modern *Homo sapiens* and the transportation of information before discussing the internet as "the most important thing since the capture of fire" (Barlow 2008).

Barlow's story of the founding of the Electronic Frontier Foundation (EFF) dates to an email he received from a young man in the Soviet Union. This man climbed under the barbed wire at the Finnish border with a cable so he could attach a modem to Finland's relatively open internet. With this contraption, this Soviet man was able to get his message out of the Soviet Union and to Barlow, writing, "We hear what you are doing to protect the American constitution on the internet, [but] what about us? We don't have a constitution." While telling this story, Barlow slapped himself in the face, saying: "It dawned on us that in cyberspace the Bill of Rights is a set of local ordinances and in cyberspace no rights can be conferred by anybody really. To the extent that rights can be conferred it is almost entirely whether or not the architecture allows for the free flow of ideas or [whether] it can be censored or constrained." Despite speaking in such sanguine and universal tones, Barlow's words were a reminder that the internet, like all networked technology, has always been territorialized, and must be read as an assemblage that includes local places, policies, and laws.

Attending Barlow's talk were Icelandic digital rights activists. They were inspired by his discussion of how tactics – techniques with technologies – are the best way to support individual and human rights in relation to the internet (Levy 1984). After a brief provocation encouraging the audience to ignore existing copyright laws, Barlow suddenly stated that his "dream for Iceland is that it could become the Switzerland of bits," that is, a country which uses its geographical sovereignty to develop laws that protect privacy. He did not elaborate on it in the lecture but did later, saying he had discussed the idea of a data haven with a government official from Monaco, stating: "I felt the answer to sovereignty was sovereignty. To fight them on their own terms" (Greenberg 2013).

Icelandic activist and poet Birgitta Jónsdóttir, sitting in the audience, heard this phrase, and after being elected to the Alþingi, the Icelandic parliament, focused on making Iceland a data haven. Jónsdóttir was a major player within WikiLeaks and is now a parliamentary minister representing the Pirate Party. She is the chair of the board of IMMI and sponsors its legislation within the Alþingi. With the collapse of their banks, and the global financial crisis of 2008, Jónsdóttir and others worked to make a data haven a reality, recognizing that the financial crisis – which began with Iceland – was tied to information markets.

In February 2015, Iceland's Supreme Court upheld convictions of market manipulation of four former executives of Kaupthing bank, with two receiving eight-month prison sentences (Scrutton & Sigurdardóttir 2015). Potentially contributing to the conviction was WikiLeaks, which on July 31, 2009 leaked a confidential document that detailed how a corrupt bank, Icesave, had irresponsibly loaned billions of euros to its shareholders (WikiLeaks 2009a). Within 24 hours, WikiLeaks had received a legal threat from Kaupthing, which was also corrupt. Jay Lim of WikiLeaks responded, "No. We will not assist the remains of Kaupthing, or its clients, to hide its dirty laundry from the global community. Attempts by Kaupthing or its agents to discover the source of the document in question may be a criminal violation of both Belgian source protection laws and the Swedish constitution. Who is your US counsel?" (WikiLeaks 2009b).

The day following the leak, RÚV, Iceland's national public-service broadcast organization, intended to cover the crisis in its major nightly newscast and reference the findings in the leak. Being gagged by a court-ordered injunction from discussing the issue, RÚV instead showed a link to the WikiLeaks page, making its editor, Julian Assange, something of a celebrity in Iceland. Kaupthing lawyers claimed that Assange deserved a year in prison for the leak. Assange soon came to Iceland to "see for himself" how legitimate this threat was (WikiLeaks 2013). There he met Jónsdóttir.

WikiLeaks had already exposed extra-judicial killings in Kenya, 500,000 intercepted pager messages on 9/11, and the dumping of 400 tons of toxic waste on behalf of Dutch commodities trader Trafigura (Stray 2010), but it was in Iceland where it was going to do its most explosive work yet. Later in 2009, Assange was invited by Icelandic information activist Smári McCarthy and others to be a speaker at the same digital rights conference in Reykjavik that John Perry Barlow spoke at a year earlier. Like Barlow before, at this conference Assange too challenged Iceland to become the Switzerland of bits.

It was likely in Iceland that Assange received the "Collateral Murder" footage that exposed the murder of Iraqi civilians by the US military and put WikiLeaks on the global map as a political force. In the video, two US AH-64 Apache helicopters direct 30 mm cannon fire at a group of 10 Iraqi men. Seven men are killed. Soon a rescue van arrives with children as passengers. The Apache strikes it, injuring the two children. Between 12 and 18 people were killed and the charge that the targets were carrying weapons proved false. It turned out that the "weapons" in question were video cameras. Assange, McCarthy, Jónsdóttir, and others worked to edit this video for publication to develop the legal argument in favor of Iceland's legal protection for journalists – the seeds of the data haven concept (figure 4.3).

McCarthy attempted to organize the information activists, Jónsdóttir selected video stills, and a fourth participant, the journalist Kristinn Hrafnsson, flew to Iraq to interview family members of those attacked in the "Collateral Murder" video. In an email to the *Guardian* that Assange wrote at the beginning of February 2010, he stated:

> I have been [in Iceland] the past few weeks advising parliamentarians here on a cross-party proposal to turn Iceland into an international "journalism haven" – a jurisdiction designed to attract organizations into publishing online from Iceland, by adopting the strongest press and source protection laws around the world. (Assange 2010; Trann 2010)

During his time in Iceland, Assange and his collaborators laid the groundwork for the data haven concept. They sought

Figure 4.3 The house in Reykjavik where WikiLeaks worked
Source: Adam Fish

to enshrine in law the freedoms they enjoyed as hacktivists that resulted in the release of the "Collateral Murder" video. Through the data haven concept and the IMMI initiatives, the former WikiLeaks volunteers were attempting to develop an assemblage that combined legal and technological elements with internet technology to support rather than threaten the freedom of the press and Icelandic citizens.

A Closer Look at the International Modern Media Institute

Following Barlow's and Assange's suggestions, McCarthy, Jóns-dóttir and colleagues began to work seriously on transforming Iceland into a data haven by bringing together the various laws that would create the most optimal conditions for protecting the storage, flow, and production of journalistic data.

Overwhelmingly, as noted above, the Icelandic parliament supported the IMMI proposals for a data haven. As Lilja

Mósesdóttir, a member of the Alþingi said of the IMMI proposals: "The main purpose is to prevent something like our financial crisis from taking place again,...they [the banks] were manipulating the news" (Stray 2010).

IMMI recognized that the financial crisis created an opportune time for change and experimentation. Its vision statement cites environmental activist Naomi Klein and her "shock doctrine" thesis about how systems of power use crises to enact controversial laws. In this vein, IMMI exists to "counter this tradition and utilize the crisis as a chance to bring about positive fundamental change" (International Modern Media Institute 2014). It was thus the breakage of the Icelandic financial system and the internet as a tool for private political communication that instigated the development of the IMMI proposals. It was from within this wreckage that IMMI sought to reconstitute a small and impactful portion of the laws and practices surrounding internet governance.

WikiLeaks, for its part, was already developing and implementing anti-surveillance and encryption technology as IMMI was attempting to implement such shifts in policy. WikiLeaks had, for instance, developed its capacity to "mirror" servers in different locations across the globe to maximize security (Fish 2016). In order to fight off legal attacks and keep its sources safe, it had "to spread assets, encrypt everything, and move telecommunications and people around the world to activate protective laws in different national jurisdictions" (Vallance 2010).

Being a target of international government surveillance and censorship led to actions whereby WikiLeaks worked to protect not only its sources but also itself. The Twitter accounts associated with WikiLeaks and Jónsdóttir have been spied on (Electronic Frontier Foundation 2011), a mole was planted in their organization (Poulsen 2013), they have been strong-armed to abandon funding after credit card companies ceased processing payments (WikiLeaks 2011), volunteers have been questioned by a grand jury, they have been hacked by GCHQ (Greenwald & Gallagher 2014), and the US Justice Department issued a warrant to seize the emails of three WikiLeaks staffers (Timm 2015).

While it is hoped that IMMI's plans and potential adoption of WikiLeaks technology would allow Icelandic data centers to be highly successful, others within Iceland are concerned that the laws would make the country susceptible to security risks. For instance, according to Jon Vilberg Gudjonsson, director of legal affairs for the Education Ministry, Iceland's foreign affairs might be jeopardized if controversial materials were stored on its shores (Chu 2011). In order to protect free speech and privacy, one part of the IMMI proposals requires Icelandic authorities to conceal IP addresses and logs. In criminal investigations, snooping, or spycraft, more powerful nations such as the United States often request or acquire such information. "We can't just say we are not bound by legal obligations or international law," said Elfa Yr Gylfadóttir, a spokeswoman for the Education Ministry, speaking against the IMMI laws (Chu 2011). Similarly, David Ardia, organizer of a citizen media law project at the Berkman Klein Center of the Harvard Law School, was skeptical about IMMI's international sovereignty and legitimacy, stating: "Obviously Iceland can't pass a law that could affect the domestic laws of another country – that changes the law in China, Pakistan, or Turkey." He continued, "Most journalism is done on the ground – it is great that servers get these protections, but it won't help local sites" (Cohen 2010).

Data Retention, Data Protection, and Intermediary Limited Liability

The previous sections have described how through the interventions of WikiLeaks, local activists, and the fortunate existence of a pro-journalist legal system, Iceland, through its IMMI initiative, represents an important case of how the new assemblages may control and manage data locally, through data havens. The IMMI proposals are a bundle of regulatory policies focused on information control. Their goal is to encourage the development of information infrastructure and laws that will dissuade legal harassment and criminal investigation.

Several elements constitute the IMMI resolutions. These include freedom of information, judicial process protection, prior restraint limitation, communications protection, source protection, judicial process protection, protection of historical records, whistleblower protection, virtual limited liability companies, statute of limitation of publishing liabilities, protection of intermediaries, protection from libel tourism, data retention laws, data protection laws, and an Icelandic Prize for Freedom of Expression. Of these we focus on three factors that are responsible for regulating intermediaries and infrastructure: *data retention, intermediary limited liability,* and *data protection.* Our interest in highlighting these is to identify the specificity of legal and regulatory factors that shape the assemblage that IMMI represents and its potential for success in combatting systems of information surveillance and control.

Data retention

Communications between sources, whistleblowers, hacktivists, and journalists generally require the use of telecommunications intermediaries like internet service providers (ISPs) and private data storage facilities. Current Icelandic telecommunications law no. 81/2003 implements the European Economic Area's mandated data retention law 2002/58/EB. These national and extra-territorial laws dictate that ISPs retain records of all traffic for six months. These laws, however, have been highly controversial. Since the terrorist attacks in Madrid in 2004 and London in 2005, the European Union (EU) has redoubled its efforts to collect and retain information. The result was the Data Retention Directive or Directive 2006/24/EC, which required ISPs in member states to extend the existing policy to retain data for 24 months. It also gave police and security agencies the power to request access to metadata details such as IP addresses, the times of emails that were sent, and more. This prompted mass protests in the EU, which included over 50,000 protesters in Berlin in 2009 and 2010 as well as mass petitions supporting legal challenges to the directive (Hintz 2013: 160).

In a letter to Cecilia Malmström, European Commissioner for Home Affairs, 86 signatories from leading EU digital rights organizations stated: "[S]uch invasive surveillance of the entire population is unacceptable" (Breyer et al. 2010). This is consistent with the IMMI's position, which would ideally remove data retention by voiding clause 2 of article 42 in the Icelandic Telecommunication Act.

IMMI has drafted a bill for parliament to remove the data retention directive from Icelandic law. This law, it claims, violates principles of proportionality, undermines privacy, and requires internet intermediaries like data centers to indiscriminately store data in case of the presence of a retroactive warrant. It argues that following the EU data retention dictates is costly and undermines the public's trust.

Intermediary limited liability

Intermediaries that mediate the experience of accessing information and using technology within Iceland include ISPs, online search engines, web hosts, interactive websites, cyber cafés, telecommunications carriers, and data centers. They are often enrolled by governments to control internet access as "proxy censors" (Kreimer 2006: 16; cited in Hintz 2013: 150). This mode of control through proxy intermediaries is particularly alarming for those involved in public, citizen, and activist media as they lack the resources to legally defend themselves from lawsuits (Hintz 2013: 151). IMMI's proposed intermediary limited liability protections provide these companies with legal protection from liability for content or communications that happen through the use of their services. This approach argues that an intermediary cannot be responsible for conducting surveillance into communications, censoring content, or monitoring users.

Articles 12–14 of the EU's Electronic Commerce Directive 2000/31/EC regulate intermediaries by treating them as "mere conduits" that transmit information. A "mere conduit" is defined as a service that (a) does not initiate the transmission; (b) does not select the receiver of the transmission; and (c) does not select or modify the information contained in the transmission. The IMMI laws would also provide indemnity for services which host or cache information.

Data protection

Since the revelations associated with Edward Snowden in 2013, personal data protection has become an increasing concern in the worlds of business, government, and civil society. A spate of 2015 court cases illustrate the increased intensity of this issue. For example, a privacy commission in Belgium sued Facebook for tracking non-users and logged-out users for advertising purposes claiming that the social media platform "trampl[ed]" over Belgian and European privacy laws (Gibbs 2015). Facebook eventually won the case on appeal. (Reuters 2016). Another case, *Vidal-Hall v. Google*, ruled that users of Google in the United Kingdom can be financially compensated for emotional stress associated with being tracked by browser cookies (Drinkwater 2015).

Another example is the case of Austrian Max Schrems, who has successfully brought a lawsuit against Facebook in the Court of Justice of the European Union in Luxembourg. The court has agreed that the collaboration between US intelligence agencies and Facebook through programs such as PRISM, as revealed by Snowden, is illegal (Powles 2015). The United States is no longer considered a "safe harbour" for European data, according to this ruling, meaning that EU companies can no longer maintain their extra-territorial practice of storing information about EU citizens in the US. This will likely instigate a growth in the EU data center industry and could be of benefit to the data center industry in Iceland compliant with these new regulations.

In light of these cases and emergent regulations, IMMI represents a pathway forward whose popularity is growing. As territoriality and jurisdiction increasingly overlap in assemblages that attempt to protect personal data and privacy, an opportunity exists to imagine an internet interwoven with the cultural, political, and legal rights of different places and communities.

Data Entrepreneurialism and Data Centers

At the 26th Chaos Computer Club meeting on December 27, 2009, Assange and Daniel Domscheit-Berg, two of the original conceivers of WikiLeaks, took the stage to introduce WikiLeaks 1.0 and the concept of Iceland as a data haven. Data centers, running on inexpensive and green Icelandic energy, could work within the IMMI model to be "the new business model for Iceland," the duo claimed (Domscheit-Berg 2009).

An integral component of the Icelandic data haven assemblage is socially minded entrepreneurialism. It is envisioned that publishers and those responsible for publishing websites would relocate to Iceland (Cohen 2010). Start-ups might ease the financial burden of insurance by relocating their data storage needs to Iceland (Babbage 2010). Others agree, claiming that if the IMMI laws are passed, "then data centers powered by Iceland's renewable energy sources could, in the future, make the country a haven for defending freedom and transparency of information, rather than a tax haven for concealing financial secrets" (Pedersen 2010). Identifying "services, start-ups, data centers, ISPs, and human rights organizations" as potential beneficiaries, the proposal "could be a lever for the economy and create new work employment opportunities," reads IMMI's website. Assange has stated that IMMI "is likely to encourage the international press and internet start-ups to locate their services" in Iceland (Vallance 2010).

The North Atlantic – Finland, Sweden, Ireland, Iceland – has become a favourite location for Facebook, Google, and Amazon data centers because the region promises access to inexpensive energy, arctic temperatures that cool computers, stable governments, tax incentives, and close proximity to almost a billion people. Through working with the data center industry, these nations hope to see increased international commerce, local business development, employment opportunities, and the immigration of skilled workers. It is thus not far-fetched for these nations to see themselves as continued beneficiaries of the data storage industry.

Considering issues of energy use, regulation, and interconnectivity to and from the island, Icelandic scholars – one of whom worked with Assange (McCarthy) – have examined how ideal Iceland would be as a location for the data center industry (McCarthy & Saitta 2012). The cold climate, liberal government, abundant green energy, and other factors make Iceland an optimal choice, with major players like the UK-based Verne Global company now establishing massive data centers on the island. That said, limited interconnectivity via sparse submarine fiber-optic cables, and the potential for EU regulations to limit the industry, may challenge Iceland's capacity to become the "Switzerland of bits" (Bücking 2014).

Extra-territorial Surveillance: Seizure and Policing of Servers

Having argued for the potential and importance of the Icelandic case and IMMI as a privacy and freedom-supporting assemblage "after the internet," we now point to the limits and challenges it faces. We note that the simple reterritorialization of the internet that the data havens and IMMI represent is not in itself sufficient. This is due to the continued presence of extra-territorial technical, legal, and political power. In that sense, a deep reterritorialization of the internet is itself a myth like so many others this book describes.

Because they are necessary to the functioning of information activism and darknet business, servers are often targets for extra-territorial seizure, where institutions and security agencies from countries like the United States operate outside of their national borders and jurisdiction to apprehend their adversaries. Servers involved in political projects have been seized before, often for suspicious reasons (Hintz 2013). For instance, the FBI seized the servers of the UK's Independent Media Center in 2004, and police seized the servers in Bristol in 2005. In 2006 and again in 2014, the Pirate Bay servers were raided in Stockholm.

In 2006, there was a raid on servers hosted by PRQ (not an abbreviation), a Swedish ISP and web hosting company founded by Fredrik Neij and Gottfrid Svartholm, two of the founders of the aforementioned Pirate Bay website. PRQ is a free speech operation with resilient technology and access to experienced legal counsel that will host data regardless of content. The 2006 raid executed by the Swedish police forces for breach of copyright was likely at the behest of the US Motion Picture Association of America (MPAA) (King 2006). Despite this loss of hardware, the Pirate Bay website was running again the next day. It was reported that they had moved new servers to a "mountain cave" outside of the city of Malmö in southern Sweden (Ernesto 2011).

WikiLeaks has kept its servers distributed and backed up across a number of different locations, including Belgium, France, Iceland, the United States, and Sweden (WikiLeaks

2013). The Swedish data center used by WikiLeaks is likely Bahnhof, a "bullet-proof hosting" company 30 meters below the earth's surface in a Cold War-era nuclear bunker. These efforts, according to WikiLeaks, were "an explicit undertaking designed to make WikiLeaks uncensorable" (WikiLeaks 2013; see also MacAskill 2010; Sutter 2010; Wakefield 2010). Physically distributed and decentralized, the location of hardware and resources makes these organizations more resilient yet also partially detectable, as the Pirate Bay discovered again on December 9, 2014 when Swedish police raided the data center where the site was allegedly hosted and seized 50 servers (Andy 2015). As data requires material hardware to remain accessible, the location of data centers will continue to be important in the data politics of the future.

We have briefly alluded to the issues of extraterritorial law trampling upon privacy and digital rights. This has affected not only the cases we describe above, but also this chapter's primary focus of Iceland. The seizure by the FBI in 2014 of a server containing information about the darknet contraband-dealing site Silk Road from the Thor Advania data center outside of Reykjavik shows the limits of the IMMI proposals, namely the shortcomings it faces in terms of enforceability and sovereignty.

The Silk Road was an anonymous peer-to-peer darknet site that enabled illicit consumption and trade. While nothing in the IMMI proposals suggests that it is designed to protect drug dealing online, the case still provides a glimpse into how foreign security and policing agencies can do as they wish. Indeed, a closer look at how US federal investigators located the server and then took hold of it in partnership with Icelandic authorities shows how unsecure data can be regardless of where it is stored. It points to how the digital rights and privacy assemblage of Iceland must continue to adapt, respond, and acquire new components to fight the hegemony of surveillance and policing.

The case against Silk Road "mastermind" Ross Ulbricht has been predicated upon the seizures and searches of the site's server. The defense has argued that the way the "state" discovered the location of the server is suspicious and has not been appropriately disclosed. Without more evidence into how the US government conducted its investigation with the

Icelandic government's assistance, the data collected by the aforementioned mysterious methods is null and void, claims the defense (*USA vs. Ulbricht* 2014). Ulbricht and lawyers have argued that all the data seized by investigators is illegally obtained and without warrant. The prosecution disagrees and has successfully argued its case. FBI agent Christopher Tarbell has claimed that his agency discovered the Silk Road's IP address by entering "miscellaneous" data into its the CAPTCHA box on the login page. The CAPTCHA – the collection of letters and numbers used to filter out spambots – was loading directly from the Thor Advania data center in Iceland, the location of the server hosting the Silk Road. The server being overseas exempted the investigators from the need to obtain a "warrant to search the server, whether for its IP address or otherwise" (Greenberg 2014). Yet, consistent with other positions, American Civil Liberties Union lawyer Jennifer Granick disagrees with the legality of this maneuver. She has stated that if an American citizen and an American investigator are involved, then the Fourth Amendment guaranteeing rights against unlawful search and seizure must apply (Greenberg 2014).

Several scholars of cybersecurity seriously doubt the claims made by Tarbell. An approach more aggressive than merely entering "miscellaneous" content into the login might have been borrowed from the methods of hackers to force the Silk Road login page to reveal its IP address. The state might have employed some of the *edgework* practices of the hacktivist assemblage we describe in this book's second chapter.

After looking at the investigator's logs, cybersecurity expert Nicholas Weaver suggests that they show that the FBI got an IP address not from a leaky CAPTCHA but rather from a PHPAdmin configuration page. This argument would support the claim that the FBI was using hacker tactics of applying command lines, essentially forcing the site to make public otherwise private information, and therefore, according to Weaver, in agreement with Granick, clearly violating the Fourth Amendment's prohibition of unlawful searches (Kravets 2014).

Thus, even with the passage of the IMMI proposals, data activists and businesses both need to be clandestine, using tactics that will keep their activities hidden from state or criminal forces that would seek to disrupt their practices. The

Silk Road case reveals that a privacy- and rights-supporting assemblage like that which we describe emerging from Iceland cannot merely rest on the legal and political aspects of territoriality. It must also use technical and tactical forms of expertise, hiding the location of its physical hardware as well as the digital means by which it can be infiltrated. Extraterritoriality thus still threatens the protections afforded by local place.

Conclusion

The concept of a data haven in Iceland demonstrates the importance of where the cloud touches ground. We have discussed how data centers reconfigure local landscapes while concretizing specific vectors of transnational connection. In doing so, these centers and their associated politics shift senses of identity and place, allowing, for example, a relatively marginal North Atlantic island to reposition itself as the center of a new world. Unlike the myth of the internet as a smooth space of frictionless flows, we see how it is actually striated with uneven terrain, an assemblage that appears to be more of a tangle than an ordered array. This chapter has shown how difference and power are woven as the internet traverses through physical landscapes and legal jurisdictions.

Since Iceland's spectacular financial crash of 2008, and the subsequent protests that kicked the government out of office, information technology and politics have cropped up in many projects of reform, and spread to other nations across the EU. The politics of information freedom, then, have been taken up in a range of ways: for example, the so-called "crowd-sourced constitution," Iceland's ongoing connections with WikiLeaks, and, most recently, the election of 10 Pirate Party MPs in 2016 – the first Pirates elected to a national parliament in the world.

These new political leaders will be advancing the idea of a data haven. By passing "information-friendly" legislation (favoring free speech, online privacy, and intermediary liability protection) and building data centers where information can live (an easy sell in Iceland thanks to the cool climate and inexpensive geothermal power). In this way, Iceland is an example of the positive benefits of a "splinternet," a fragmented internet of striation and difference. After a period of mythologizing the power of the internet to create global unification, and amidst the present concerns of surmounting the information inequality of the digital divide, this chapter shares the importance of learning from territoriality and locality. The IMMI proposals are one example of a small nation using its jurisdictional autonomy to challenge an increasingly hegemonic internet dominated by American companies and governmental agencies.

However captivating it may be, the idea of "another internet" might obscure the nature of Iceland's actual innovations. While some internet activists are indeed experimenting with alternatives, many information activists in Iceland are making clever changes to what they have, modifying and customizing already-existing systems – whether through legal "hacks" like IMMI, or by building more publicly accessible tools for encryption. Anthropologists and science and technology studies scholars have long talked about infrastructures as complex co-productions between political ambitions, aesthetic ideals, everyday encounters, and material things. Many Icelandic information activists share this view, and use it to take apart and tweak what most of us take for granted when we accept the internet "as is."

Moving beyond trivializing metaphors of weightless clouds, this chapter revamps assumptions about the internet by emphasizing the materiality, economics, and politics of cloud computing. Contemporary research is beginning to exhibit how geographic location, state jurisdictions, local economics, and culturally specific policies regarding copyright and privacy impact how computing clouds are situated not in the sky but in specific localities. Technology-minded entrepreneurs, politicians, and engineers make the point that Iceland is an ideal data haven because it has the coldest latitude, greenest power, best Atlantic geography, highest encryption standards, a restabilized liberal economy, and a left-libertarian political culture. Exploiting some of these conditions, WikiLeaks worked from Iceland to release its first shocking revelations. In this way, Icelandic data activists are showing the world the cultural form for a progressive cloud infrastructure. Instead of being a "breakage" of the internet, Iceland's fragmentation is fertile ground for experiments in technologically assisted democracy.

This conclusion returns us to the theme of the book: how local and vernacular cultures of activism shape assemblages after the existing internet. Yet it is also a reminder that this chapter's case of situating the internet within an assemblage with *national policy, extra-legal attempts to capture and manipulate data,* and a *cultural vision of social liberalism* does not guarantee privacy or digital rights. As we see through this chapter's illustration of how forces of territoriality and extra-territoriality clash, the assemblages shaped to support this vision must be dynamic, heterogeneous, nomadic, and ever adaptive.

Coda

Cultural values and beliefs, judicial and legal systems, national policies, environmental and economic factors, political histories – this book's chapters have urged us to view these in tandem and interaction with the internet. The internet, too, consists of a convergence of technological, legal, historical, and cultural forces.

According to the theory of assemblage that ties together the cases in this book, the internet should be understood not as a unified totality or infrastructure. Such a myth is dangerous, as it blocks alternative imaginaries of networked technology in line with grassroots communities while instead embracing an increasingly opaque utopia that serves the interests of the elite few. In contrast, the assemblages we share in this book describe the internet relative to heterogeneous parts, interaction, and contradiction.

In order to make sense of a complicated system, myths erase complexity. They obfuscate as much as they reveal. They hide the rich technical and social aspects of the internet from public view. Instead, we must view technologies as part of material infrastructures, bringing social and technical assemblages into conversation with the voices, belief systems, and values of users and communities.

The actors we describe in our chapters disassemble the internet they experience and generate local assemblages that bring technical and non-technical components together as they struggle against systems of hegemony. Native American and Oaxacan indigenous people, discussed in chapter 1, have developed their own digital networks to support their values, knowledge practices, and aspirations as they struggle for economic and cultural autonomy. Hacktivists, described in chapter 2, attempt to exploit a disassembled internet by finding and mining its fissures in order to perform politically motivated operations. Yet their attempts to recover a myth of the internet as decentralized and autonomous are challenged by extra-legal technology and political practices across the world. The Mosireen activist collective of Egypt, discussed in chapter 3, move past the existing internet by taking their content offline. Instead they support nomadic activities such as the projection of revolutionary narratives into public spaces. They recognize the potential in shifting how and where content is shared without maintaining a reliance on the internet. And finally, the International Modern Media Institute (IMMI) example discussed in chapter 4 reveals the possibility of storing data locally and securely, an *intranet* of sorts, which would be subject to the geographically specific laws of Iceland. Though the IMMI case promotes the possibility of a data haven, data centers in Iceland may still be targets for various forms of surveillance. In a sense, this final case study attempts to rescue the internet "as is" while still falling short of securing the goal of data privacy.

This book started with the assumption in chapter 1 that the internet is an open assemblage of non-unitary parts. In direct contrast with the theories of Deleuze and assemblage theory, internet mythologies attempt to discursively constitute this space of difference as friction-free, unifying, and standing for dominantly Western ideals that marry capitalism with democracy. Our examples juxtapose troubling realities alongside utopic myths. We do note in our chapters, however, that while it may be advantageous to work within the margins of the internet through the crafting of local assemblages, this may in turn block the possibility for larger-scale, viral change. This is the paradox of scale: progressive networking experiments may succeed in providing communicative voice on a small scale, only to exponentially grow and soon be used for surveillance, privacy invasion, and other issues that ultimately stifle voice in the public sphere. The paradox works in the opposite direction as well: projects that refuse to scale remain closed and insular, unable to enter the public sphere.

Our chapters reveal this paradox. In secluding images of their cultural patrimony in private online repositories, the Zuni community featured in chapter 1 may maintain an insularity that challenges the ability to transform larger systems of power. In attacking corporatism, the hacktivists we describe in chapter 2 are forced to face the force of the militarized police state and its incarcerating institutions. In conducting street video-screenings, the Mosireen media activists of Egypt of chapter 3 short-change the robust online audiences they once had across the world. And in leveraging the territoriality of the small island of Iceland, IMMI described in chapter 4 may still be easily overwhelmed by external political, technological, and economic forces.

Our examples are taken from the margins of political, economic, and social hegemony in an unequal world. This world is fueled by an internet powered by multibillion-dollar corporations and surveillance-oriented nation-states. The communities each chapter describes produce assemblages that represent a pragmatic critique of both the empirical internet and internet-centric scholarship. In this way, they, as well as this book, attempt to reassemble the internet as a space conducive for progressive democratic agendas.

Yet the very bases of success for the actors we describe, their creative crafting of local assemblages, may also hamper their ability to counter the hegemonies against which they struggle. The space for activism that the protagonists of each chapter represent can only be articulated as at the margins of political, economic, and cultural hegemony. In this sense, the situated, small-scale assemblages that we present are limited by their specificity. Our chapters show how the internet can be acted upon relative to particular times, places, tools, and contexts. In this sense, we reveal how the internet is not a monolithic entity but subject to a recursive process of disassembly and reassembly.

Each chapter of this book describes a battle against a far more powerful force: cultural institutions and telecommunications corporations that objectify and silence the voices of indigenous peoples (chapter 1); extra-judicial systems of policing (chapter 2); draconian Western-backed authoritarian regimes of the Middle East (chapter 3); and corporations and governments that exploit technology to support surveillance of internet users (chapter 4). Each of the forces our protagonists oppose are far more powerful than the grassroots adversaries we discuss.

These systems of power constrain our discourse, and therefore maintain the marginalization of those whose stories we share. Indigenous and non-Western peoples are seen through the lens of an exoticized past, lacking agency or control over their destiny. Hackers are falsely seen as lawless and anarchistic rude-boys with no respect for the property of others. The Middle East is mistakenly seen as a terror-ridden part of the world that is devoid of democratic voices and where democratic activism may be replaced by fundamentalist forces like ISIS. And Icelandic data entrepreneurs and activists are seen as irrelevant.

Such is not enough to achieve our far more ambitious aims of helping bring together professionals, activists, and scholars interested in a world "after the internet" that is transformative rather than thoroughly fragmented. We thus wonder whether the local stories we share in each case can give way to transformative, dynamic, and power-uprooting movements that are far larger in scale and viral in possibility, ones that may recover some of the original ideals and visions with which the internet was associated, or give birth to new larger-scale narratives that are not altogether new yet inspiring.

What, then, can we imagine an internet "after the internet" to look like?

First, it seems critical that *technological components* crafted at the grassroots can be applied more widely to support diverse internet users across the world. Our discussion of fluid ontologies and autonomous infrastructures in chapter 1, uses of encrypted browsers such as TOR and darknet technologies in chapter 2, video, media, and network manipulation techniques in chapter 3, and local legal statutes in chapter 4 reveal a number of judicial, design, and engineering interventions that can work with the potential scale of the global internet while supporting sovereignty and voice on the level of a user community.

Second, we believe that there is great value in *intervening within existing political economies* associated with the internet.

The passage of net-neutrality legislation in the United States – now threatened by President Trump – was an important moment that challenged already-existing dynamics that disproportionately favored wealthy and corporate individuals and institutions. We must push further with public interest legislation and advocacy across the world to recover the internet's potential to serve as a global public space, recognizing that every public space must provide the opportunity for participants to be who they are, to be true to their cultural, social, and individual identities rather than bow to bourgeois theories of the rational actor. A number of grassroots, anti-austerity movements have revealed the power of internet use in ways that support such public interest, as we discuss in the context of media activism within chapter 3. Associated with this, we must challenge the corporatization of web platforms and networks, knowing the perils of following the path of television and newspaper industries that have been acquired by a limited number of monopolistic holding companies, such as News Corp, Time Warner, and Disney. Challengers, private or public, must emerge to Google and Facebook's ownership over the means by which data is gathered, owned, monetized, and ordered. We must develop critical literacy to recognize how information shared on digital networks may be captured, retained, and aggregated to support political and economic agendas far removed from our control.

A new internet is possible "after the internet." It, too, will be an assemblage, yet, unlike what today's internet has become, it will no longer need to objectify or exploit the voices of its users across the world.

References

Abaza, M. 2013. Cairo Diary: Space-Wars, Public Visibility and the Transformation of Public Space in Post-revolutionary Egypt. In *Public Space, Media Space*. Palgrave Macmillan UK.

Adelman, C. 1989. The Practical Ethic Takes Priority over Methodology. In W. Carr (Ed.), *Quality in Teaching: Arguments for a Reflective Profession*. Brighton: Falmer Press.

Aitkenhead, D. 2013. Julian Assange: The Fugitive. *Guardian*. http://www.theguardian.com/media/2012/dec/07/julian-assange-fugitive-interview

Al-Anani, K. 2008. *Brotherhood in Egypt: Gerontocracy Fighting Against the Clock*. Cairo: Dar Al-shourouk.

Al-Rawi, A. K. 2014. The Arab Spring and Online Protests in Iraq. *International Journal of Communication*, 8(1): 916–42.

Altman, I. 1975. The Environment and Social Behavior: Privacy, Personal Space, Territory, and Crowding. http://eric.ed.gov/?id=ED131515

Anderson, B., M. Kearnes, C. McFarlane, & D. Swanton. 2012. On Assemblages and Geography. *Human Geography*, 2(2): 171–89.

Anderson, C. 2008. The End of Theory: The Data Deluge Makes the Scientific Method Obsolete. *Wired*. http://www.wired.com/science/discoveries/magazine/16-07/pb_theory

Anderson, J. E. 2009. *Law, Knowledge, Culture: The Production of Indigenous Knowledge in Intellectual Property Law*. Cheltenham: Edward Elgar Publishing.

Andrejevic, M. 2009. Privacy, Exploitation and the Digital Enclosure. *Amsterdam Law Forum*, 1(4): 47–62.

Andrejevic, M. 2013. *Infoglut: How Too Much Information is Changing the Way We Think and Know*. New York: Routledge.

Andy. 2015. Police Seized 50 Servers in Pirate Bay Raid. Torrent Freak. https://torrentfreak.com/police-seized-50-servers-in-pirate-bay-raid-150123/

Appadurai, A. 1990. Difference and Disjuncture in the Global Cultural Economy. *Theory, Culture & Society*, 7(2): 295–310.

Arquilla, J. 2013. Last War Standing. *Foreign Policy*, August 13. http://foreignpolicy.com/2013/08/13/last-war-standing/

Assange, J. 2010. Creating a Media Haven in Iceland. WikiLeaks, February 7. https://facthai.wordpress.com/2010/02/07/creating-a-media-haven-in-iceland-wikileaks/

Assange, J. 2013. The Banality of "Don't Be Evil." *New York Times*, June 1. http://www.nytimes.com/2013/06/02/opinion/sunday/the-banality-of-googles-dont-be-evil.html

Assange, J. 2014. Who Should Own the Internet? *New York Times*, December 4. http://www.nytimes.com/2014/12/04/opinion/julian-assange-on-living-in-a-surveillance-society.html

Austin-Holmes, A. Forthcoming. *From Revolution to Coup: Mass Risings in Egypt against the Mubarak Regime, the Military Junta, and the Muslim Brotherhood.* Book manuscript in progress.

Babbage. 2010. The Switzerland of Bits. *The Economist*, June 17. http://www.economist.com/blogs/babbage/2010/06/icelands_media_law

Badone, E. 2004. Crossing Boundaries: Exploring the Borderlands of Ethnography, Tourism, and Pilgrimage. In E. Badone & S. R. Roseman (Eds.), *Intersecting Journeys: The Anthropology of Pilgrimage and Tourism.* Urbana: University of Illinois Press.

Bamford, J. 2012. The NSA Is Building the Country's Biggest Spy Center (Watch What you Say). *Wired*, 15 March. http://www.wired.com/2012/03/ff_nsadatacenter/all/1

Barad, K. 2003. Posthumanist Performativity: Toward an Understanding of How Matter Comes to Matter. *Signs: Journal of Women in Culture and Society*, 28(3): 801–31.

Barlow, J. P. 1996, A Declaration of the Independence of Cyberspace. Electronic Frontier Foundation. https://www.eff.org/cyberspace-independence

Barlow, J. P. 2008. John Perry Barlow on the Right to know. *Forbes*. https://www.youtube.com/watch?v=snQrNSE1T7Y

Barthes, R. 2000. *Mythologies*. Trans. A. Lavers. London: Vintage.

Bell, J. A., K. Christen, & M. Turin. 2013. Introduction: After the Return. *Museum Anthropology Review*, 7(1–2): 1–21.

Bellware, K. 2016. Internet Access Isn't Just A Tech Issue. It's A Civil Rights Issue. *The Huffington Post*, May 23. http://www.huffingtonpost.com/entry/detroit-internet-access_us_57430e6fe4b045cc9a716b6d

Bennett, W. L., & A. Segerberg. 2012. The Logic of Connective Action: Digital Media and the Personalization of

Contentious Politics. *Information, Communication & Society*, 15(5): 739–68.

Bergson, H. 1932. *The Two Sources of Morality and Religion*. Trans. R. A. Audra & W. H. Carter. Garden City, NY: Doubleday.

Beyer, J., & F. McKelvey. 2015. You Are Not Welcome Among Us: Pirates and the State. *International Journal of Communication*, 9: 890–908.

Bigo, D. 2000. When Two Become One: Internal and External Securitisations in Europe. In M. Kelstrup & M. Williams (Eds.), *International Relations Theory and the Politics of European Integration: Power, Security and Community*. London: Routledge.

Blas, Z. 2014. Contra-Internet Aesthetics. In O. Kholeif (Ed.), *You Are Here: Art After the Internet*. Manchester: Cornerhouse Publications.

Blum, A. 2012. *Tubes: A Journey to the Center of the Internet*. New York: HarperCollins.

Bort, R. 2015. The Tech Industry is Stripping San Francisco of Its Culture, and Your City Could be Next. *Newsweek*, October 1. http://www.newsweek.com/san-francisco-tech-industry-gentrification-documentary-378628

Bourdieu, P. 1977. *Outline of a Theory of Practice*. Trans. R. Nice. Cambridge and New York: Cambridge University Press.

Bourdieu, P. 1990. *The Logic of Practice*. Trans. R, Nice. Cambridge: Polity.

Boyd, D., & K. Crawford. 2012. Critical Questions for Big Data: Provocations for a Cultural, Technological, and Scholarly Phenomenon. *Information, Communication, & Society*, 15(5): 662–79.

Breyer, P., & 106 other authors. 2010. Letter to Cecilia Malmström, European Commissioner for Home Affairs. 22 June. http://www.vorratsdatenspeicherung.de/images/DRletter_Malmstroem.pdf

Brooks, J., & I. A Boal. 1995. Introduction. In J. Brooks. & I. A. Boal, (Eds.), *Resisting the Virtual Life: The Culture and Politics of Information*. San Francisco: City Lights.

Brunton, F., & H. Nissenbaum. 2013. Political and Ethical Perspectives on Data Obfuscation. In M. Hildebrandt & K. de Vries (Eds.), *Privacy, Due Process and the Computational Turn: The Philosophy of Law Meets the Philosophy of Technology*. New York. Routledge.

Bücking, J. 2014. Data Protection, Data Security, and Compliance Using the Example of Iceland. Verne Global. https://verneglobal.com/uploads/2016/10/4795b676-8450-67d3-687b-448fe0ca9023/data-protection-data-security-and-compliance-ex-iceland2015.pdf

Butler, J. 1997. *The Psychic Life of Power: Theories in Subjection*. Stanford: Stanford University Press.

Byrne, D. 2013. The Internet Will Suck All Creative Content Out of the World. *Guardian*. http://www.theguardian.com/music/2013/oct/11/david-byrne-internet-content-world

Calabrese, A. 2004. Virtual Nonviolence? Civil Disobedience and Political Violence in the Information Age. *info*, 6(5): 326–38.

Carey, J. 2002. A Cultural Approach to Communication. In D. McQuail (Ed.), *McQuail's Reader in Mass Communication Theory*. London: Sage.

Carr, N. G. 2010. *The Shallows: What the Internet is Doing to Our Brains*. New York: W. W. Norton.

Castells, M. 1996. *The Rise of the Network Society*. Oxford: Blackwell.

Castells, M. 2000. The Rise of the Fourth World. In D. Held & A. McGrew (Eds.), *The Global Transformations Reader: An Introduction to the Globalization Debate*. Oxford: Blackwell.

Castells, M. 2009. *Communication Power*. Oxford: Oxford University Press.

Chhabra, E. 2016. Social Enterprise Accelerator Solvey Gets Over 3 Million Views on YouTube. *Forbes*, June 4. http://www.forbes.com/sites/eshachhabra/2016/06/04/social-enterprise-accelerator-solvey-gets-over-3-million-views-on-youtube/

Chipchase, J. 2007. The Anthropology of Mobile Phones. TED Talk, March. https://www.ted.com/talks/jan_chipchase_on_our_mobile_phones

Christen, K. A. 2012. Does Information Really Want to be Free? Indigenous Knowledge Systems and the Question of Openness. *International Journal of Communication*, 6: 2870–93.

Chu, H. 2011. Iceland Seeks to Become Sanctuary for Free Speech. *Los Angeles Times*, April 2. http://articles.latimes.com/2011/apr/02/world/la-fg-iceland-free-speech-20110403

Ciborra, C. 2002. *The Labyrinths of Information: Challenging the Wisdom of Systems*. Oxford: Oxford University Press.

Cleaver, H. 1998. The Zapatistas and the Electronic Fabric of Struggle. http://la.utexas.edu/users/hcleaver/zaps.html

Clifford, J. 1989. The Others: Beyond the "Salvage" Paradigm. *Third Text*, 3(6): 73–8.

Cluley, G. 2011. British Police Issue Warning to Hacktivists. Naked Security by Sophos, August 3. https://nakedsecurity.sophos.com/2011/08/03/british-police-issue-warning-to-internet-hacktivists/

Cohen, J., & E. Schmidt. 2013. *The New Digital Age: Reshaping the Future of People, Nations and Business*. London: Hachette UK.

Cohen, N. 2010. A Vision of Iceland as a Haven for Journalists. *New York Times*, February 21. http://www.nytimes.com/2010/02/22/business/media/22link.html

Coleman, E. G. 2003. The (Copylefted) Source Code for the Ethical Production of Information Freedom. In *Sarai Reader 2003: Shaping Technologies*. New Delhi: Sarai, New Media Initiative.

Coleman, E. G. 2010. Ethnographic Approaches to Digital Media. *Annual Review of Anthropology*, 39: 487–505.

Coleman, E. G. 2014. *Hacker, Hoaxer, Whistleblower, Spy*. London: Verso.

Coleman, E. G., & A. Golub. 2008. Hacker Practice: Moral Genres and the Cultural Articulation of Liberalism. *Anthropological Theory*, 8(3): 255–77.

Collier, S. J., & A. Ong (Eds.). 2004. *Global Assemblages: Technology, Politics, and Ethics as Anthropological Problems*. Oxford: Wiley-Blackwell.

Colvin, N. The Logic of Leaks, Reconsidered. *Limn*, 8. http://limn.it/the-logic-of-leaks-reconsidered/

Costanza-Chock, S. 2012: Mic Check! Media Cultures and the Occupy Movement. *Social Movement Studies: Journal of Social, Cultural and Political Protest*, 11(3–4): 375–85.

Couldry, N. 2010. *Why Voice Matters: Culture and Politics After Neoliberalism*. London: Sage.

Couldry, N. 2013. A Necessary Disenchantment: Myth, Agency and Injustice in a Digital World. Inaugural Lecture, London School of Economics and Political Science, 21 November. http://www.lse.ac.uk/media@lse/documents/MPP/Nick-Couldrys-LSE-INAUGURAL-SCRIPT.pdf

Couldry, N., & H. Jenkins (Eds.). 2014. Participations: Dialogues on the Participatory Promise of Contemporary Culture and Politics. *International Journal of Communication*, 8 (Forum): 1107–12.

Courage Foundation n.d. Discovery SIGINT Targeting Scenarios and Compliance. https://edwardsnowden.com/2014/02/18/discovery-sigint-targeting-scenarios-and-compliance/

Cox, J. 2015. Ashley Madison Hackers Speak Out: "Nobody was Watching." Motherboard, August 21. http://motherboard.vice.com/read/ashley-madison-hackers-speak-out-nobody-was-watching

Crovitz, G. 2012. Who Really Invented the Internet? *Wall Street Journal*, July 22. http://online.wsj.com/article/SB10000872396390444464304577539063008406518.html

Cubitt, S. 2016. *Finite Media: Environmental Implications of Digital Technology*. Durham, NC: Duke University Press.

Cubitt, S., R. Hassan, & I. Volkmer. 2011. Does Cloud Computing Have a Silver Lining? *Media, Culture & Society*, 33(1): 149–58.

Curran, J. 2012. Reinterpreting the Internet. In J. Curran, D. Freeman, & N. Fenton (Eds.), *Misinterpreting the Internet*. London: Routledge.

Daskal, J. 2015. The Un-Territoriality of Data. *Yale Law Journal,* http://papers.ssrn.com/sol3/papers.cfm?abstract_id=2578229##

DeLanda, M. 2006. *A New Philosophy of Society: Assemblage Theory and Social Complexity.* London: A&C Black.

Deleuze, G. 1994. *Difference and Repetition.* Trans. P. R. Patton. New York: Columbia University Press.

Deleuze, G. 2007. Eight Years Later. In *Two Regimes of Madness: Texts and Interviews 1975–1995.* Trans. A. Hodges & M. Taormina. New York: Semiotext(e).

Deleuze, G., & F. Guattari. 1983. *Anti-Oedipus: Capitalism and Schizophrenia.* Trans. R. Hurley, M. Seem, & H. R. Lane. Minneapolis: University of Minnesota Press.

Deleuze, G., & F. Guattari. 1987. *A Thousand Plateaus: Capitalism and Schizophrenia.* Trans. B. Massumi. Minneapolis: University of Minnesota Press.

Della Porta, D., M. Andretta, L. Mosca, & H. Reiter. 2006. *Globalization from Below: Transnational Activists and Protest Networks.* Minneapolis: University of Minnesota Press.

DeNardis, L. 2012. Hidden Levers of Internet Control: An Infrastructure-Based Theory of Internet Governance. *Information, Communication & Society,* 15(5): 720–38.

Department of Justice. 2015. Former Federal Agents Charged with Bitcoin Money Laundering and Wire Fraud. http://www.justice.gov/opa/pr/former-federal-agents-charged-bitcoin-money-laundering-and-wire-fraud

Derrida, J. 1978. *Writing and Difference.* Trans. A. Bass. Chicago: University of Chicago Press.

Deuze, M. 2007. *Media Work.* Cambridge: Polity.

Diaz, J. 2012. These Breasts Nailed a Hacker for the FBI. Gizmodo, April 12. http://gizmodo.com/5901430/these-breasts-nailed-anonymous-hacker-in-fbi-case

DiMaggio, P., E. Hargittai, C. Celeste, & S. Shafer. 2004. Digital Inequality: From Unequal Access to Differentiated Use. In K. M. Neckerman (Ed.), *Social Inequality.* New York: Russell Sage Foundation.

Domscheit-Berg, D. 2009. WikiLeaks Release 1.0. 26th Chaos Computer Communication Congress. https://events.ccc.de/congress/2009/Fahrplan/events/3567.en.html

Drinkwater, D. 2015. Google–Vidal-Hall "Opens the Floodgates" to Data Breach Compensation. *SC Magazine,* May 15. https://www.scmagazineuk.com/google-vidal-hall-opens-the-floodgates-to-data-breach-compensation/article/537060/

Eagleton, T. 2003. *After Theory.* London: Penguin.

Earl, J., & K. Kimport. 2011. *Digitally Enabled Social Change: Activism in the. Internet Age,* Cambridge, MA: MIT Press.

The Economist. 2010. The Data Deluge. *The Economist*, February 25. http://www.economist.com/node/15579717

Electronic Frontier Foundation. 2011. Privacy Loses in Twitter/WikiLeaks Records Battle. Electronic Frontier Foundation, November 10. https://www.eff.org/press/releases/privacy-loses-twitterwikileaks-records-battle.

Emirbayer, M. 1997. Manifesto for Relational Sociology. *American Journal of Sociology* 103: 281–317.

Ernesto. 2011. The Pirate Bay Ships New Servers to Mountain Complex. Torrent Freak. https://torrentfreak.com/the-pirate-bay-ships-new-servers-to-mountain-complex-110516/

Eskander, W. 2013. Egypt's Kazeboon: Countering State Narrative. Middle East Institute, July 12. http://www.mei.edu/content/egypts-kazeboon-countering-state-narrative

Evans, W. 2016. Cyberspace is the Child of the Industrial Age: Defining it as Independent is Nonsense. Institute for Ethics and Emerging Technologies, February 20. http://ieet.org/index.php/IEET/more/evans0220

Farivar, C. 2015. Judge Sets 71-Month Sentence for Former Ssecret Service Agent Who Plundered Silk Road. Ars Technica, December 8. http://arstechnica.co.uk/tech-policy/2015/12/rogue-secret-service-agent-who-stole-from-silk-road-sentenced-to-nearly-6-years/

Filippi, P. De, & S. McCarthy. 2012. Cloud Computing: Centralization and Data Sovereignty. *European Journal of Law and Technology*, 3(2). http://ejlt.org/article/view/101/234

Fish, A. 2015 Who Really Benefits from the Internet Space Race? The Conversation, June 18. https://theconversation.com/who-really-benefits-from-the-internet-space-race-43425

Fish, A. 2016. Mirroring the Videos of Anonymous: Cloud Activism, Living Networks, and Political Mimesis. *Fiberculture Journal*, 26(191): 85–107.

Fish, A. 2017a. Scalia.warhead1: Securitization Discourse in Hacktivist Video. In J. Vuori & R. Saugmann (Eds.), *Visual Security Studies: Sights and Spectacles of Insecurity and War*. New York: Routledge.

Fish, A. 2017b. *Technoliberalism and the End of Participatory Culture in the United States*. New York: Palgrave Macmillan.

Fish, A., & L. Follis. 2015. Edgework, State Power, and Hacktivists, *Hau: Journal of Ethnographic Theory*, 5(2): 383–90.

Fish, A., & L. Follis. 2016. Gagged and Doxed: Hacktivism's Self-Incrimination Complex. *International Journal of Communication*, 10: 3281–300.

Fish, A., & R. Srinivasan. 2012. Digital Labor is the New Killer App. *New Media & Society*, 14(1): 137–52.

Follis, L., & A. Fish. 2017. Half-Lives of Hackers and the Shelf Life of Hack. *Limn*, 8. http://limn.it/half-lives-of-hackers-and-the-shelf-life-of-hacks/

Fox10. 2011. Social Media and Self-Incrimination. Fox10Phoenix.com, April 16. http://www.fox10phoenix.com/news/arizona-news/120954429-story

Fuchs, C. 2007. *Internet and Society: Social Theory in the Information Age*. New York: Routledge.

Fuchs, C. 2015. *Culture and Economy in the Age of Social Media*. New York: Routledge.

Fukuyama, F. 1992. *The End of History and the Last Man*. New York: Free Press.

Furlong, K. 2011. Small Technologies, Big Change: Rethinking Infrastructure Through STS and Geography. *Progress in Human Geography*, 35(4): 460–82.

García, C., M. von Bülow, J. Ledezma, & P. Chauveau. 2014. What Can Twitter Tell Us About Social Movements' Network Topology and Centrality? Analysing the Case of the 2011–2013 Chilean Student Movement. *International Journal of Organisational Design and Engineering*, 3(3–4): 317–37.

Geismar, H. 2005. Copyright in Context: Carvings, Carvers, and Commodities in Vanuatu. *American Ethnologist*, 32(3): 437–59.

Gerbaudo, P. 2012. *Tweets and the Streets: Social Media and Contemporary Activism*. London: Pluto Press.

Gibbs, S. 2015. Belgium takes Facebook to Court Over Privacy Breaches and User Tracking. *Guardian*, June 15. http://www.theguardian.com/technology/2015/jun/15/belgium-facebook-court-privacy-breaches-ads

Giddens, A. 1984, *The Constitution of Society: Outline of Structuration Theory*. Cambridge: Polity.

Giddens, A. 1994. *Beyond Left and Right: The Future of Radical Politics*. Cambridge: Polity.

Gillespie, T., P. J. Boczkowski, & K. A. Foot. 2014. *Media Technologies: Essays on Communication, Materiality, and Society*. Cambridge, MA: MIT Press.

Ginsburg, F. 2008. *Rethinking the Digital Age: The Media and Social Theory*. New York: Routledge.

Gladwell, M. 2012. Small Change: Why the Revolution Will Not Be Tweeted. *The New Yorker*, October 4 http://www.newyorker.com/reporting/2010/10/04/101004fa_fact_gladwell?currentPage=all

Goel, V. 2015. Facebook Strives to Bring Cheap Wi-Fi to Rural India. *New York Times* Bits Blog, October 25. http://bits.blogs.nytimes.com/2015/10/25/facebook-strives-to-bring-cheap-wi-fi-to-rural-india-2/

Goldsmith, J., & T. Wu. 2006. *Who Controls the Internet?* Oxford: Oxford University Press.

Gonzales, R. G. 2008. Left Out But Not Shut Down: Political Activism and the Undocumented Student Movement. *Northwestern Journal of Law and Social Policy*, 3(2): 219–39.

Goodwin, J., & J. M. Jasper. 1999. Caught in a Winding, Snarling Vine: The Structural Bias of Political Process Theory. *Sociological Forum*, 14(1): 27–54.

Gore, A. 1991. Infrastructure for the Global Village. *Scientific American*, 265(3): 150–3.

Gore, A. 1994. Speech delivered at the Information Superhighway Summit at UCLA January 11. http://www.uibk.ac.at/voeb/texte/vor9401.html

Graham, M. 2011. Time Machines and Virtual Portals: The Spatialities of the Digital Divide. *Progress in Development Studies*, 11(3): 211–27.

Graham, S., & S. Marvin. 2001. *Splintering Urbanism: Networked Infrastructures, Technological Mobilities and the Urban Condition.* Hove: Psychology Press.

Greenberg, A. 2013. *This Machine Kills Secrets: How WikiLeakers, Hacktivists, and Cypherpunks are Freeing the World's Information.* London: Virgin Books.

Greenberg, A. 2014. Feds "Hacked" Silk Road without a Warrant? Perfectly Legal, Prosecutors Argue. *Wired*, July 10. http://www.wired.com/2014/10/feds-silk-road-hack-legal/

Greenberg, A. 2016. It's Been 20 Years Since This Man Declared Cyberspace Independence. *Wired*, February 8. https://www.wired.com/2016/02/its-been-20-years-since-this-man-declared-cyberspace-independence/

Greenwald, G. 2014. How Covert Agents Infiltrate the Internet to Manipulate, Deceive, and Destroy Reputations. The Intercept, February 24. https://theintercept.com/2014/02/24/jtrig-manipulation/

Greenwald, G., & R. Gallagher. 2014. Snowden Documents Reveal Covert Surveillance and Pressure Tactics Aimed at WikiLeaks and Its Supporters. The Intercept, February 18. https://theintercept.com/2014/02/18/snowden-docs-reveal-covert-surveillance-and-pressure-tactics-aimed-at-wikileaks-and-its-supporters/

Grossman, L. 2004. 10 Questions for Bill Gates. *Time*, February 29. http://content.time.com/time/magazine/article/0,9171,596122,00.html

Guadamuz, A. 2016. 20 years of the Declaration of Independence of Cyberspace. TechnoLlama, February 10. http://www.technollama.co.uk/20-years-of-the-declaration-of-independence-of-cyberspace

Guzman-Concha, C. 2012. The Students' Rebellion in Chile: Occupy Protest or Classic Social Movement? *Social Movement Studies*, 11(3–4): 408–15.

Habermas, J. 1985. Civil Disobedience: Litmus Test for the Democratic Constitutional State. *Berkeley Journal of Sociology*, 30(1): 95–116.

Hacktivism: Online Covert Action. 2012. https://snowdenarchive.cjfe.org/greenstone/collect/snowden1/index/assoc/HASH01b7/cc3bf79e.dir/doc.pdf

Hafner, K., and M. Lyon. 1996. *Where Wizards Stay Up Late: The Origins of the Internet*. New York: Simon & Schuster.

Hargittai, E. 2007. Whose Space? Differences Among Users and Non-Users of Social Network Sites. *Journal of Computer-Mediated Communication*, 13(1): 276–97.

Hargittai, E. 2008. The Digital Reproduction of Inequality. In D. Grusky (Ed.), *Social Stratification*. Boulder, CO: Westview Press.

Hargittai, E., & Y. P. Hsieh 2013. Digital Inequality. In W. H. Dutton (Ed.), *Oxford Handbook of Internet Studies*. Oxford: Oxford University Press.

Harvey, D. 1990. *The Condition of Postmodernity: An Enquiry into the Origins of Cultural Change*. Oxford: Blackwell.

Harvey, D. 2001. *Spaces of Capital: Towards a Critical Geography*. Edinburgh: Edinburgh University Press.

Haseloff, A. M. 2005. Cybercafés and Their Potential as Community Development Tools in India. *The Journal of Community Informatics*, 1(3). http://ci-journal.net/index.php/ciej/article/view/226

Hassanpour, N. 2011. Media Disruption Exacerbates Revolutionary Unrest: Evidence from Mubarak's Natural Experiment. Paper presented at the American Political Science Association 2011 Annual Meeting, September 1–4, Seattle, WA. https://papers.ssrn.com/sol3/papers.cfm?abstract_id=1903351

Hayes, E. N., & T. Hayes. 1970. *Claude Lévi-Strauss: The Anthropologist as Hero*. Cambridge, MA: MIT Press.

Hayles, N. K. 1999. *How We Became Posthuman: Virtual Bodies in Cybernetics, Literature, and Informatics*. Chicago: University of Chicago Press.

Hebdige, D. 1984. *Subculture: The Meaning of Style*. New York: Methuen.

Heidegger, M. 1954. The Question Concerning Technology. In C. Hanks (Ed.), *Technology and Values: Essential Readings*. Oxford: Wiley-Blackwell, 2010.

Hill, K. 2013. Blueprint of NSA's Ridiculously Expensive Data Center in Utah Suggests It Holds Less Info Than Thought. *Forbes*, July 24. http://www.forbes.com/sites/kashmirhill/2013/07/24/

blueprints-of-nsa-data-center-in-utah-suggest-its-storage-capacity-
is-less-impressive-than-thought/#a4600c31c85a

Hintz, A. 2013. Dimensions of Modern Freedom of Expression: WikiLeaks, Policy Hacking, and Digital Freedoms. In A. Hintz, B. Benedetta, & M. Patrick (Eds.), *Beyond WikiLeaks: Implications for the Future of Communications, Journalism and Society.* Basingstoke: Palgrave Macmillan.

Hogan, M. 2013, "Bumblehive" and "Sealand": Big Data Infrastructures. Culture Digitally, November 25. http://culturedigitally.org/2013/11/bumblehive-and-sealand-big-data-infrastructures/

Hogan, M. 2015. Water Woes and Data Flows: The Utah Data Center. *Big Data and Society*, 2(2): 1–12.

Holt, J., & P. Vonderau. 2015. "Where the Internet Lives": Data Centers as Cloud Infrastructure in Signal Traffic. In L. Parks & N. Starosielski (Eds.), *Signal Traffic: Critical Studies of Media Infrastructures.* Champaign: University of Illinois Press.

Howard, P. N. 2010. *The Digital Origins of Dictatorships and Democracy: Information Technology and Political Islam.* New York: Oxford University Press.

Howard, P. N., L. Busch, & P. Sheets. 2010. Comparing Digital Divides: Internet Access and Social Inequality in Canada and the United States. *Canadian Journal of Communication*, 35(1): 109–28.

Howard, P. N., & M. Hussain. 2013. *Democracy's Fourth Wave? Digital Media and the Arab Spring.* New York: Oxford University Press.

Hu, T.-h. 2015. *A Prehistory of the Cloud.* Cambridge, MA: MIT Press.

Ingold, T. 2000. *The Perception of the Environment: Essays on Livelihood, Dwelling and Skill.* Hove: Psychology Press.

Ingold, T. 2007. Materials Against Materiality. *Archaeological Dialogues*, 14(1): 1–16.

The Intercept. 2014. Full Spectrum Cyber Effects. April 4. https://theintercept.com/document/2014/04/04/full-spectrum-cyber-effects/

International Modern Media Institute. 2014. Vision. https://en.immi.is/about-immi/vision/

Jackson, S. J. 2014. Rethinking Repair. In T. Gillespie, P. Boczkowski, & K. Foot (Eds.), *Media Technologies: Essays on Communication, Materiality and Society.* Cambridge, MA: MIT Press.

Jasanoff, S. 2004. *States of Knowledge: The Co-production of Science and the Social Order.* London and New York: Routledge.

Jenkins, H. 2006. *Convergence Culture: Where Old and New Media Collide.* New York: New York University Press.

Jenkins, H., R. Puroshotma, K. Clinton, M. Weigel, & A. J. Robison 2005. Confronting the Challenges of Participatory Culture: Media

Education for the 21st Century. John D. and Margaret T. MacArthur Foundation. http://www.newmedialiteracies.org/wp-content/uploads/pdfs/NMLWhitePaper.pdf

Jessop, B. 2012. The World Market, Variegated Capitalism, and the Crisis of European integration. In P. Nousios, H. Overbeek, & A. Tsolakis (Eds.), *Globalisation and European Integration: Critical Approaches to Regional Order and International Relations*. London: Routledge.

Johnson, S. 2012. The Internet? We Built That. *New York Times*, September 21. http://www.nytimes.com/2012/09/23/magazine/the-internet-we-built-that.html?pagewanted=all

JTRIG n.d. The Art of Deception: Training for a New Generation of Covert Online Operations. https://edwardsnowden.com/wp-content/uploads/2014/02/the-art-of-deception-training-for-a-new.pdf

Jurgenson, N. 2012. The IRL Fetish. *The New Inquiry*, June 28. http://thenewinquiry.com/essays/the-irl-fetish/

Kakabadse, A., N. K. Kakabadse, & A. Kouzmin. 2003. Reinventing the Democratic Governance Project Through Information Technology? A Growing Agenda for Debate. *Public Administration Review*, 63(1): 44–60.

Keen, A. 2007. *The Cult of the Amateur: How Today's Internet is Killing Our Culture*. New York: Crown Business/Doubleday/Random House.

Keen, A. 2015. *The Internet is Not the Answer*. New York: Atlantic Monthly Press.

Khalikova, D., & A. Fish. 2016. Networked Idiots: Affective Economies and Neoliberal Subjectivity in Russian Viral Video. *Global Media and Communication*, 12(2): 143–59.

Khamis, S., P. B. Gold, & K. Vaughn. 2012. Beyond Egypt's "Facebook Revolution" and Syria's "YouTube Uprising": Comparing Political Contexts, Actors and Communication Strategies. *Arab Media & Society*, 15, http://www.arabmediasociety.com/?article=791

King, J., director. 2006. *Steal This Film*. Producer: The League of Noble Peers.

Kirsch, J., H. Moltke, J. Appelbaum, L. Poitras, M. Ermert, & C. Grothoff. 2014. NSA/GCHQ: The HACIENDA Program for Internet Colonization. C't, August 15. https://www.heise.de/ct/artikel/NSA-GCHQ-The-HACIENDA-Program-for-Internet-Colonization-2292681.html?hg=1&hgi=8&hgf=false

Kitchin, R., & P. J. Hubbard. 1999. Research, Action, and "Critical" Geographies. *Area*, 31(3): 195–8.

Kittler, F. 1994. Unconditional Surrender. In H.-U. Gumbrecht & K. L. Pfeiffer (Eds.), *Materialities of Communication*. Stanford: Stanford University Press.

Kravets, D. 2014. US Says It Can Hack into Foreign-Based Servers without Warrants. Ars Technica, October, 7. http://arstechnica.com/tech-policy/2014/10/us-says-it-can-hack-into-foreign-based-servers-without-warrants/

Kreimer, S. F. 2006. Censorship by Proxy: The First Amendment, Internet Intermediaries, and the Problem of the Weakest Link. *University of Pennsylvania Law Review*, 155(11): 11–101.

Kreiss, D. 2011. Open Source as Practice and Ideology: The Origin of Howard Dean's Innovations in Electoral Politics. *Journal of Information Technology & Politics*, 8(3): 367–82.

Lanier, J. 2010. *You Are Not a Gadget: A Manifesto*. New York: Alfred A. Knopf.

Latour, B. 1996. *Aramis, or, The Love of Technology*. Trans. C. Power. Cambridge MA: Harvard University Press.

Leiderman, J. 2013. Justice for the PayPal WikiLeaks Protestors: Why DDoS is Free Speech. *Guardian*, January 22. http://www.theguardian.com/commentisfree/2013/jan/22/paypal-wikileaks-protesters-ddos-free-speech

Leopold, T. 2013. Author: Think Twice About "the Internet." CNN, July 19. http://edition.cnn.com/2013/07/19/tech/web/morozov-internet-save-everything/

Lévi-Strauss, C. 1978. *Myth and Meaning: Cracking the Code of Culture*. New York: Routledge & Kegan Paul.

Levin, A. 2015. Life After Ashley Madison: How to Operate in a World without Secrets. *The Huffington Post*, August 19. http://www.huffingtonpost.com/adam-levin/life-after-ashley-madison_b_8011500.html

Levy, S. 1984. *Hackers: Heroes of the Computer Revolution*. New York: Anchor Press.

LOVELY HORSE n.d. https://snowdenarchive.cjfe.org/greenstone/collect/snowden1/index/assoc/HASH6dce.dir/doc.pdf

Lyng, S. 2005 Edgework and the Risk-Taking Experience. In S. Lyng (Ed.), *Edgework: The Sociology of Risk-Taking*. Abingdon and New York: Routledge.

Lyng, S., & R. Matthews. 2007. Risk, Edgework, and Masculinities. In K. Hannah-Moffat & P. O'Malley (Eds.), *Gendered Risks*. Milton Park: Routledge-Cavendish.

MacAskill, E. 2010. WikiLeaks Website Pulled by Amazon after US Political Pressure. *Guardian*, December 2. http://www.theguardian.com/media/2010/dec/01/wikileaks-website-cables-servers-amazon

Madianou, M. 2015. Digital Inequality and Second-Order Disasters: Social Media in the Typhoon Haiyan Recovery. *Social Media + Society*, 1(2). http://journals.sagepub.com/doi/full/10.1177/2056305115603386

Manjoo, F. 2012. Obama Was Right: The Government Invented the Internet. Slate, July 24. http://www.slate.com/articles/technology/technology/2012/07/who_invented_the_internet_the_outrageous_conservative_claim_that_every_tech_innovation_came_from_private_enterprise_.html

Mann, M. 2012. *The Sources of Social Power III*. Cambridge: Cambridge University Press.

Mansell, R. 1990. Rethinking the Telecommunication Infrastructure: The New "Black Box." *Research Policy*, 19(6): 501–15.

Marcus, G.E., & E. Saka, 2006. Assemblage. *Theory, Culture & Society*, 23(2–3): 101–9.

Martinez, E., & A. García. 2000. *What is "Neo-Liberalism"? A Brief Definition*. New York: The New Press.

Marwick, A. E., D. Murgia-Diaz, & J. G. Palfrey. 2010. Youth, Privacy and Reputation (Literature Review). SSRN Scholarly Paper. Rochester, NY: Social Science Research Network, April 12. http://papers.ssrn.com/abstract=1588163

Massey, D. B. 2005. *For Space*.London: Sage.

Massumi, B. 1987. Translator's Foreword: Pleasures of Philosophy. In G. Deleuze & F. Guattari. *A Thousand Plateaus: Capitalism and Schizophrenia*. Trans. B. Massumi. Minneapolis: University of Minnesota Press.

Maxwell, R., & T. Miller. 2012. *Greening the Media*. Oxford: Oxford University Press.

Mayer, J. 2013. What's the Matter with Metadata? *The New Yorker*, June 6. http://www.newyorker.com/news/news-desk/whats-the-matter-with-metadata

Mayer-Schönberger, V., & K. Cukier. 2013. *Big Data: A Revolution That Will Transform How We Live, Work and Think*. London: John Murray.

McAdam, D. 1982. *Political Process and the Development of Black Insurgency, 1930–1970*. Chicago: University of Chicago Press.

McCarthy, S., & E. Saitta. 2012. Islands of Resilience: Comparative Model for Energy, Connectivity, and Jurisdiction, Realizing European ICT Possibilities Through a Case Study of Iceland. Prepared at the Request of The Greens/European Free Alliance in the European Union, IMMI Research Report. https://www.greens-efa.eu/files/doc/docs/afb325f24f941eb3c5b2b5307d149ba2.pdf

McCracken, H. 2012. How Government Did (and Didn't) Invent the Internet. *Time*, July 25. http://techland.time.com/2012/07/25/how-government-did-and-didnt-invent-the-internet/

McLuhan, M. 1964. *Understanding Media*. New York: McGraw-Hill.

Melber, A. 2011. Malcolm Gladwell Surfaces to Knock Social Media in Egypt. *The Nation*, February 2. http://www.thenation.com/blog/158241/malcolm-gladwell-surfaces-knock-social-media-egypt

Meyer, D. S., & D. C. Minkoff. 2004.Conceptualizing Political Opportunity. *Social Forces*, 82(4): 1457–92.

Miller, D., & D. Slater. 2000. *The Internet: An Ethnographic Approach*. Oxford: Berg. http://techland.time.com/2012/07/25/how-government-did-and-didnt-invent-the-internet/

Mollerup, N., & S.Gaber. 2015. Making Media Public: On Revolutionary Street Screenings in Egypt. *International Journal of Communication*, 9: 2903–21.

Morozov, E. 2011. *The Net Delusion: The Dark Side of Internet Freedom*. New York: Public Affairs Books.

Morozov, E. 2013. *To Save Everything, Click Here: The Folly of Technological Solutionism*. New York: Basic Books.

Mosco, V. 2004. *The Digital Sublime: Myth, Power, and Cyberspace*. Cambridge, MA: MIT Press.

Mosco, V. 2014. *To the Cloud: Big Data in a Turbulent World*. Boulder, CO: Paradigm Press.

Moyers, B. 2014. Anatomy of the Deep State. Moyers & Company, February 21, http://billmoyers.com/2014/02/21/anatomy-of-the-deep-state/

Moyers, B., & J. Campbell. 1988. *The Power of Myth* (ed. B. S. Flowers). New York: Doubleday.

Musiani, F. 2012. Caring About the Plumbing: On the Importance of Architectures in Social Studies of (Peer-to-Peer) Technology. *Journal of Peer Production*, 1(online). http://peerproduction.net/issues/issue-1/peer-reviewed-papers/caring-about-the-plumbing/

Musil, S. 2014. Sony Hack Leaked 47,000 Social Security Numbers, Celebrity Data. CNet. http://www.cnet.com/news/sony-hack-said-to-leak-47000-social-security-numbers-celebrity-data/

Nah, S., & D. S. Chung. 2016. Communicative Action and Citizen Journalism: A Case Study of OhmyNews in South Korea. *International Journal of Communication*, 10: 2297–317.

Nahon, K. 2014. Fighting for Which Future? When Google Met WikiLeaks. Culture Digitally, September 18. http://culturedigitally.org/2014/09/fighting-for-which-future-when-google-met-wikileaks/

Nakashima, E. 2015. Chinese Hack of Federal Personnel Files Including Security-Clearance Database. *The Washington Post*, June 12. https://www.washingtonpost.com/world/national-security/chinese-hack-of-government-network-compromises-security-clearance-files/2015/06/12/9f91f146-1135-11e5-9726-49d6fa26a8c6_story.html

Nasdaq. 2013. Data Centers: Nucleus of the Digital Universe. Nasdaq, December 3. https://seekingalpha.com/article/1874791-data-centers-the-nucleus-of-the-digital-universe

Naude, J. H. 2009. Technological Singularity and Transcendental Monism: Co-producers of Sustainable Alternative Futures. *Journal of Futures Studies*, 13(3): 49–58.

Nemer, D., & G. Freeman. 2015. Empowering the Marginalized: Rethinking Selfies in the Slums of Brazil. *International Journal of Communication*, 9: 1832–47.

Nicholson, R. 2015. Is the Ashley Madison Hack Another Step Towards a Post-Embarrassment World? *Guardian*, July 24. http://www.theguardian.com/commentisfree/2015/jul/24/is-the-ashley-madison-hack-another-step-towards-a-post-embarrassment-world

NSA, 2010. INTOLERANT: Who Else Is Targeting Your Target? Collecting Data Stolen by Hackers. https://snowdenarchive.cjfe.org/greenstone/collect/snowden1/index/assoc/HASH017f/1cdc5958.dir/doc.pdf

NSA. 2014. New Collection Posture. https://www.aclu.org/files/natsec/nsa/20140722/New%20Data%20Collection%20Posture.pdf

Ong, A., & S. J. Collier. 2005. *Technological Assemblages: Technology, Politics, and Ethics as Anthropological Problems*. Oxford: Wiley-Blackwell.

Ortner, S. 1978, *Sherpas Through Their Rituals*. Cambridge: Cambridge University Press.

Page, L. 2014. Where Is Google Going Next? TED, March. http://www.ted.com/talks/larry_page_where_s_google_going_next/transcript?language=en

Pagliery, J. 2015. Now You Can Search the Ashley Madison Cheaters List. CNN, August 19. http://money.cnn.com/2015/08/19/technology/ashley-madison-search/

Palermo, E, & P. Wagenseil. 2015. 10 Worst Data Breaches of All Time. Tom's Guide, December 14. http://www.tomsguide.com/us/biggest-data-breaches,news-19083.html

Parks, L. 2013. Mapping Orbit: Toward a Vertical Public Space. In C. Berry, J. Harbord, & R. O. Moore (Eds.), *Public Space, Media Space*. New York: Palgrave Macmillan.

Parks, L., & N. Starosielski. 2015. *Signal Traffic: Critical Studies of Media Infrastructures*. Urbana: University of Illinois Press.

Patelis, K., & P. Hatzopoulos. 2013. Understanding Social Media Monopolies. *First Monday*, 18(3). http://firstmonday.org/ojs/index.php/fm/article/view/4614/3418

Pedersen, R. 2010. Icelanders Hope to Host Controversial Data from Around the World. IDG News Service, March 12. http://news.idg.no/cw/art.cfm?id=C28ED506-1A64-6A71-CE4C7D8EF77CC5FC

Perez, E., & S. Prokupecz. 2015. First on CNN: US Data Hack May be 4 Times Larger Than the Government Originally Said. CNN, June 24. http://edition.cnn.com/2015/06/22/politics/opm-hack-18-milliion/

Philip, K., L. Irani, & P. Dourish. 2010. Postcolonial Computing: A Tactical Survey. *Science, Technology & Human Values*, 37(1): 3–29.

Pickering, A. 2010. *The Mangle of Practice: Time, Agency, and Science.* Chicago: University of Chicago Press.

Postill, J. 2011. *Localizing the Internet: An Anthropological Account.* Oxford and New York: Berghahn.

Postman, N. 1993. *Technopoly.* New York: Vintage Books.

Poulsen, K. 2013. WikiLeaks Volunteer was a Paid Informant for the FBI. *Wired*, June 27,. http://www.wired.com/2013/06/wikileaks-mole/all/

Powles, J. 2015. Data Privacy: The Tide is Turning in Europe – But is It Too Little, Too Late? *Guardian*, April 6. http://www.theguardian.com/technology/2015/apr/06/data-privacy-europe-facebook.

Qiang, X. 2011. The Battle for the Chinese Internet. *Journal of Democracy*, 22(2): 47–61.

Rainsford, S. 2011. Anger as Spanish Police Move on Barcelona Protest Camp. BBC, 28 May. http://www.bbc.co.uk/news/av/world-europe-13582863

Reich, R. 1991. The Stateless Manager. *Best of Business Quarterly*, Fall: 85–91.

Rentz, C. 2015. Video Spotlights Freddie Gray at Baker and Mount Streets. *The Baltimore Sun*, May 20. http://www.baltimoresun.com/news/maryland/sun-investigates/bs-md-mount-baker-streets-20150520-story.html

Rethemeyer, R. K. 2007. The Empires Strike Back: Is the Internet Corporatizing Rather Than Democratizing Policy Processes? *Public Administration Review*, 67(2): 199–215.

Reuters 2016. Facebook Just Won a Legal Battle Over Privacy in This European Court. *Forbes*, June 29. http://fortune.com/2016/06/29/facebook-belgium-data/

Richards, B. 1993. Technophobia and Technophilia. *British Journal of Psychotherapy*, 10(2): 188–95.

Risen, J., & L. Poitras. 2014. NSA Collecting Millions of Faces from Web Images. *The New York Times*, June 1. http://www.nytimes.com/2014/06/01/us/nsa-collecting-millions-of-faces-from-web-images.html

Ronfeldt, D. & J. Arquilla. 2001. Networks, Netwars, and the Fight for the Future. *First Monday*, 6(10). http://firstmonday.org/ojs/index.php/fm/article/view/889/798

Rosaldo, R., H. Calderón, & J. D. Salvadívar (Eds.). 1991. *Criticism in the Borderlands: Studies in Chicano Literature, Culture and Ideology.* Durham, NC: Duke University Press.

Sack, R. 1983. Human Territoriality: A Theory. *Annals of the Association of American Geographers*, 73(1): 55–74.

Sandvig, C. 2013. Connection at Ewiiaapaayp Mountain. In L. Nakamura & P. Chow-White (Eds.), *Race After the Internet*. New York: Routledge

Sargsyan, T. 2016) Data Localization and the Role of Infrastructure for Surveillance, Privacy, and Security. *International Journal of Communication*, 10(17): 2221–37.

Sassen, S. 1998. On the Internet and Sovereignty. *Indiana Journal of Global Legal Studies*, 5(2): 545–59.

Sassen, S. 2002. Towards a Sociology of Information Technology. *Current Sociology*, 50(3): 365–88.

Sassen, S. 2004. Local Actors in Global Politics. *Current Sociology*, 52(4): 649–70.

Sauter, M. 2014. *The Coming Swarm*. New York: Bloomberg.

Sawhney, H. 1992a. Demand Aggregation Strategies for Rural Telephony. *Telecommunications Policy*, 16(2): 167–78.

Sawhney, H. 1992b. The Public Telephone Network: Stages in Infrastructure Development. *Telecommunications Policy*, 16(7): 538–52.

Sawhney, H. 1992c. Rural Telephone Companies: Diverse Outlooks and Shared Concerns. *Telecommunications Policy*, 16(1): 16–26.

Sawhney, H., J. Ehrlich, S. Hwang, D. Phillips, & L. Sung. 1991. Small Rural Telephone Companies, Cooperatives, and Regional Alliances. In J. Schmandt, F. Williams, R. H. Wilson, & S. Strover (Eds.), *Telecommunications and Rural Development: A Study of Private and Public Sector Innovation*. New York: Praeger.

Schiller, D. 2000. *Digital Capitalism*. Cambridge, MA: MIT Press.

Schone, M., R. Esposito, M. Cole, & G. Greenwald. 2014. Exclusive: Snowden Docs Show UK Spies Attacked Anonymous, Hackers. NBC News, 5 February. http://www.nbcnews.com/feature/edward-snowden-interview/exclusive-snowden-docs-show-uk-spies-attacked-anonymous-hackers-n21361

Scola, N. 2014. White House names Google's Megan Smith the next Chief Technology Officer of the United States. *The Washington Post*, September 4. https://www.washingtonpost.com/news/the-switch/wp/2014/09/04/white-house-names-googles-megan-smith-the-next-chief-technology-officer-of-the-united-states/?utm_term=.cb7513c7ebae

Scott, J. C. 1998 *Seeing Like a State: How Certain Schemes to Improve the Human Condition Have Failed*, New Haven: Yale University Press.

Scrutton, A., & R. Sigurdardóttir. 2015. Iceland Convicts Bad Bankers and Says Other Nations Can Act. Reuters, February 13. http://uk.reuters.com/article/uk-iceland-bankers-idUKKBN0LH00C20150213

Sennett, R. 1977. *The Fall of Public Man*, New York: Knopf.

Sennett, R. 2008. *The Craftsman*. New Haven: Yale University Press.

Shirky, C. 2008 *Here Comes Everybody: The Power of Organizing without Organizations*. New York: Penguin Press.

Shirky, C. 2011. The Political Power of Social Media: Technology, the Public Sphere Sphere, and Political Change. *Foreign Affairs*, 90(1): 28–41.

Shome, R. 2006. Thinking Through the Diaspora: Call Centers, India, and a New Politics of Hybridity. *International Journal of Cultural Studies*, 9(1), 105–24.

Silverstone, R., & L. Haddon. 1996. Design and the Domestication of ICTs: Technical Change and Everyday Life. *Communicating by Design: The Politics of Information and Communication Technologies*, 44–74.

Singer, N. 2013. Axiom Lets Consumers See Data It Collects. *New York Times*, September 4. http://www.nytimes.com/2013/09/05/technology/acxiom-lets-consumers-see-data-it-collects.html

Singh, P. J. 2010. From a Public Internet to the Internet Mall. *Economic and Political Weekly*, XLV(42): 17–19.

Soja, E. 1989. *Postmodern Geographies: The Reassertion of Space in Critical Social Theory*. London: Verso.

Solove, D. J. "I've Got Nothing to Hide" and Other Misunderstandings of Privacy. SSRN Scholarly Paper. Rochester, NY: Social Science Research Network, July 12. http://papers.ssrn.com/abstract=998565

Spivack, N. 2013. The Post-Privacy World. *Wired*. http://www.wired.com/insights/2013/07/the-post-privacy-world/

Srinivasan, R. 2004. Tribal Peace – Preserving the Cultural Heritage of Dispersed Native American Communities. In *Proceedings of the International Conference on Cultural Heritage and Informatics*, September.

Srinivasan, R. 2006a. Indigenous, Ethnic and Cultural Articulations of New Media. *International Journal of Cultural Studies*, 9(4): 497–518.

Srinivasan, R. 2006b. Where Information Society and Community Voice Intersect. *The Information Society*, 22(5), 355–65.

Srinivasan, R. 2007. Ethnomethodological Architectures: Information Systems Driven by Cultural and Community Visions. *Journal of the American Society for Information Science and Technology*, 58(5), 723–33.

Srinivasan, R. 2010, On Slacktivism: A Letter in Response to Malcolm Gladwell's Article (October 4, 2010). *The New Yorker*, October 25. http://www.newyorker.com/magazine/2010/10/25/on-slacktivism-4

Srinivasan, R. 2012. Designing Technology to Support Non-Western Community Knowledge. http://rameshsrinivasan.org/2016/04/21/amidolanne/

Srinivasan, R. 2013. Bridges Between Cultural and Digital Worlds in Revolutionary Egypt. *The Information Society*, 29(1): 49–60.

Srinivasan R. 2014. What Tahrir Square Has Done for Social Media: A 2012 Snapshot in the Struggle for Political Power. *The Information Society*, 30(1): 71–80.

Srinivasan, R. 2017. *Whose Global Village? Rethinking How Technology Shapes Our World.* New York: New York University Press.

Srinivasan, R., J. Enote, K. M. Becvar, & R. Boast. 2009. Critical and Reflective Uses of New Media Technologies in Tribal Museums. *Museum Management and Curatorship*, 24(2): 161–81.

Srinivasan, R., & J. Huang. 2005. Fluid Ontologies for Digital Museums. *International Journal on Digital Libraries*, special issue on *Digital Museums*, 5(3): 193–204.

Stark, D. 2009. *The Sense of Dissonance: Accounts of Worth in Economic Life.* Princeton and Oxford: Princeton University Press.

Starosielski, N. 2015. *The Undersea Network.* Durham, NC: Duke University Press.

Stibel, J. 2013. *Breakpoint: Why the Web Will Implode, Search Will be Obsolete, and Everything Else You Need to Know About Technology is in Your Brain.* London: Palgrave Macmillan.

Stray, J. 2010. Iceland Aims to Have Become an Offshore Haven for Journalists and Leakers. NiemanLab. http://www.niemanlab.org/2010/02/iceland-aims-to-become-an-offshore-haven-for-journalists-and-leakers/

Streeter, T. 2003. The Romantic Self and the Politics of Internet Commercialization. *Cultural Studies*, 17(5): 648–68.

Suarez-Villa, L. 2012. *Globalization and Technocapitalism: The Political Economy of Corporate Power and Technological Domination.* London: Ashgate.

Sundaram, R. 2009. Recycling Modernity: Pirate Electronic Cultures in India. *Third Text*, 13(47): 59–65.

Sunde, P. 2015. Pirate Bay Founder: I Have Given Up. Vice News Motherboard, 11 December. http://motherboard.vice.com/read/pirate-bay-founder-peter-sunde-i-have-given-up?trk_source=popular

Sutter, J. 2010. The Technical Muscle Behind WikiLeaks. CNN, July 27. http://edition.cnn.com/2010/TECH/innovation/07/26/how.wikileaks.works/

Tilly, C. 1990. *Coercion, Capital, and European States, AD 990–1990.* Cambridge, MA: Basil Blackwell

Timm, T. 2015. The War on Leaks Has Gone Too Far When Journalists' Emails Are Under Surveillance. *Guardian*, January 25. http://www.theguardian.com/commentisfree/2015/jan/25/war-on-leaks-gone-way-too-far-journalist-emails-are-under-surveillance

Trann, M. 2010. Iceland Plans Future as Global Haven for Freedom of Speech. *Guardian*, February 12. http://www.theguardian.com/world/2010/feb/12/iceland-haven-freedom-speech-wikileaks

Tsing, A. L. 2005. *Friction: An Ethnography of Global Connection.* Princeton: Princeton University Press.

Tufekci, Z. 2011. Why the "How" of Social Organizing Matters and How Gladwell's Latest Contrarian Missive Falls Short. Technosociology. http://technosociology.org/?p=305

Turnbull, D. 2009. Working with Incommensurable Knowledge Traditions: Assemblage, Diversity, Emergent Knowledge, Narrativity, Performativity, Mobility and Synergy. http://thoughtmesh.net/publish/279.php

Ulanoff, L. 2012. Does Instagram Owe Kodak a Billion Dollar Thanks?, http://mashable.com/2012/04/10/what-does-instagram-owe-kodak/#cjUfSqvpeZqp

US District Court for the Northern District of California. 2015. Affidavit of Special Agent Tigran Gambaryan in Support of Criminal Complaint. *United States v. Carl M. Force IV and Shaun W. Bridges*, March 25 (filed).

USA vs. Ulbricht. 2014. http://www.nysd.uscourts.gov/cases/show.php?db=special&id=416

Vallance, Cs. 2010. WikiLeaks and Iceland MPs Propose "Journalism Haven." BBC, February 12. http://news.bbc.co.uk/1/hi/technology/8504972.stm

Wakefield, J. 2010. WikiLeaks' Struggle to Stay Online. BBC, December 7. http://www.bbc.co.uk/news/technology-11928899

Warschauer, M. 2004. *Technology and Social Inclusion: Rethinking the Digital Divide.* Cambridge, MA: MIT Press.

Weber, M. 1946. *Essays in Sociology* (eds. H. H. Gerth & C. W. Mills). Oxford: Oxford University Press.

Weizman, E. 2007. *Hollow Land: Israel's Architecture of Occupation.* London: Verso.

WikiLeaks. 2009a. Icesave Debt Negotiation Email Between Indriði H. Þorláksson and the IMF's Mark Flanagan. April 13. https://wikileaks.org/wiki/Icesave_debt_negotiation_email_between_Indri%C3%B0i_H._%C3%9Eorl%C3%A1ksson_and_the_IMF%27s_Mark_Flanagan,_13_Apr_2009

WikiLeaks. 2009b. Icelandic Bank Kaupthing Threat to WikiLeaks Over Confidential Large Exposure Report., July 31. https://wikileaks.org/wiki/Icelandic_bank_Kaupthing_threat_to_WikiLeaks_over_confidential_large_exposure_report,_31_Jul_2009

WikiLeaks. 2011. Banking Blockade. https://wikileaks.org/Banking-Blockade.html

WikiLeaks. 2013. We Steal Secrets: The Story of WikiLeaks. https://wikileaks.org/IMG/html/gibney-transcript.html

Winter, A., director. 2015. *Deep Web*. Producers: A. Webb, G. Zipper, & M. Schiller.

Zadrozny, B. 2015. Crime-Scene Selfies: Generally a Bad Idea. *Daily Beast*, February 9. http://www.thedailybeast.com/articles/2015/02/09/crime-scene-selfies-generally-a-bad-idea.html

Zillien, N., & E. Hargittai. 2009. Digital Distinction: Status-Specific Types of Internet Usage. *Social Science Quarterly*, 90(2): 274–91.

Zuckerberg, M. 2014.: Connecting the World from the Sky. https://fbcdn-dragon-a.akamaihd.net/hphotos-ak-ash3/t39.2365-6/851574_611544752265540_1262758947_n.pdf

Index

Abdalla, Khalid 87, 93, 100
ACORN 39
after the internet 3, 20 21,
    24, 47, 102, 133
AirBnB 8
agency 26
algorithmic mediation 13
alternative computing 51
Alphabet, Inc. 10, 11
Amidolanne 41, 42, 43, 47
Anahoho 42, 43
Anonymous 59, 67, 70
Appadurai, Arjun 29
appropriation of
    technology 76
Arab Spring 73, 75, 76
architecture of the internet 9
Arquilla, John 56–7
Ashley Madison 106–7, 139
Assange, Julian 6, 31, 50, 51,
    66, 115–16, 122, 123
assemblage(s) 17, 21, 22, 27,
    36, 43, 73, 74, 81, 84, 95,
    130, 131
assemblage theory 32

Baltimore 82
Baran, Paul 19

Barlow, John Perry 1, 2, 3,
    114
Barthes, Roland 12
Bergson, Henri 77
big data 7, 57, 108–9
black boxes infrastructures
    36
Black Lives Matter 82
Blas, Zach 17
borderland (theory of) 25
Bouazizi, Mohamed 81, 82
Brexit 10
Bridges, Shaun W. 64
Brown, Barrett 50, 61

Cairo 75
call centers 31
CAPTCHA 126
Chile 102
Chilean student
    movement 73, 82, 83
Chipchase, Jan 30
Christen, Kim 33
citizen journalism 78, 79
Clinton, Hillary 10
cloud as metaphor 14, 23,
    32, 103, 104, 108–9, 128
Cohen, Jared 11

"Collateral Murder"
    footage   116–17
Coleman, Gabriella   34
collective action   78, 79
commercialization (of
    internet)   9
Connectivity Lab   28, 29
contra-internet aesthetics   18
counternetwar   56
crackers   50

data centers   58, 103, 108–12,
    118, 121, 122, 125, 127,
    131
data haven   105, 117–19, 123
data protection   18, 22, 127
data retention   60, 120–1
Dean, Howard   16
decryption   49
DeLanda, Manuel   39
Deleuze, Gilles   6, 18, 19, 47,
    100 101, 131
deterritorialization   2
digital capitalism   110
digital divide   27, 28
digital economy   104
digital labor   8
digital piracy   3
distributed denial of service
    attack (DDoS)   69–70
domestication of
    technology   76

Eagleton, Terry   20
echo chambers   13
edgerank   65
edgework   22
Egypt   77, 102
Egyptian revolution   84, 85,
    86–7
encryption   49, 50, 67, 71
enote, Jim   40
Evans, Woody   3
e-mobilization   83

e-movements   83
e-tactics   83

Facebook   3, 8, 10, 13, 76,
    79, 84
Facebook Free Basics   29
Facebook revolution   74
FBI   58, 71, 112, 124, 125,
    126
Fish, Adam   9, 32
fluid ontology   37
Force, Carl   63–4
Foreign Affairs magazine   78
Fukuyama, Francis   15

Gaber, Sherief   85, 86, 91, 93,
    98–9, 106
Gates, Bill   4
GCHQ   67-69, 118
geeks   50
Gerbaudo, Paolo   84
Gestell   27
gift economy   7
Gladwell, Malcolm   75, 79
global village   2
Godard, Jean-Luc   100
Google   3, 10, 11, 13, 76,
    84
Google Loon   28, 29
Gore, Al   15
Gray, Freddie   82
Greenberg, Andy   2
Guadamuz, Andres   2
Guattari, Félix   6, 18, 19, 47

Habermas, Jürgen
hacking   48, 57
hacktivists   22, 131
Hamilton, Omar   91
heterarchy   57–8
human networks   39

Ibrahim, Gigi   75
Iceland   18, 104, 110–33

IMMI 11–13, 115, 117–23, 125–6, 128, 131–2
Indignados 73, 82, 83
information activism 124
infrastructures 5
Ingold, Tim 26
innovation within constraint 26
Instagram 8
intermediary limited liability 112, 120–1, 127
internet: as material 10; rhizomatic 19
internet governance institutions 3
internet relay chat (IRC) 63
internet service providers 120
intranets 113
Inuit 33
Iran's Green Revolution 82
Israeli Defense Forces (IDF) 57

Joint Threat Research Intelligence Group (JTRIG) 67
Jónsdóttir, Birgitta 115-116, 118

Kaupthing bank 115, 155
Kazeboon, Aaskar 94, 102
Kelly, Kevin 108
King, Rodney 77
Kodak 8

Las Maquidaloras 30
Live Stream 83

Manning, Chelsea 49, 50
Maspero massacre 89
McCarthy, Smári 116–17, 123
media activism 93
Microsoft 3

mirror of Narcissus (media as) 91
Mixtec 45, 46
Morozov, Evgeny 12, 79
Mosireen (collective) 84, 92, 94, 99, 102, 131, 132
Mubarak regime 79
Mukurtu 34
Mumble 83
Muslim Brotherhood 81, 100
mythologies 11, 14, 15, 26, 73, 109, 130–1

NAFTA 11
National Security Agency (NSA) 5, 6, 8, 11, 49, 57–8, 67–70, 105–6, 112
Native Americans 131
neoliberalism 10
net neutrality 7
netwar 56–7, 60, 63
No to Military Trials (Egypt) 89
North Atlantic countries 113, 123
Nunavut 33

Oaxaca 44, 46
Obama, Barack 5, 16
Occupy movement 74, 82, 83, 102
online network 91
ontological turn 37

Page, Larry 28
Papua New Guinea 25
participation 80
People's Mic 83
personal data 23, 58–62, 103–12, 121–2
Pirate Bay 69, 124-125
practice theory 77
PRISM project 5

provincialization 21; of technology 34
PRQ 124

RAND 56–7
Raven Tales 33
recommendation algorithms 84
reconstruction of technology 76
recycling of modernity 34
relationality 33
repair cultures 34
reterritorialization 124
Rhizomatica 44, 45, 46, 47
rhizomatics 93
ritual 45
ROLLING THUNDER 67, 69, 76
Ronfeldt, David 56–7

Sarkozy, Nicholas 2
Schrems, Max 122
science and technology studies (STS) 19
search algorithms 84
selfie-incrimination 22, 49, 58–64, 67, 70–1
Sepik River 25
sharing 7
Shirky, Clay 78
Silicon Valley 11
Silk Road
situating technology 12
slacktivism 5
Snowden, Edward 5
social liberalism 23
social media revolution 76
social networks 81
sociotechnical analysis 19
Spain 102
splinternet 128
Srinivasan, Ramesh 21, 25
strategic traditionalism 32
subversion of technology 76

Sunde, Peter 4
Swartz, Aaron 49

Tahrir Cinema 91, 92, 95
Tahrir Square 75, 81, 87
technodeterminism 24
technological components 21, 133
technoliberal culture 2
technology and inequality 10
technophilia 12
TED 28
Toque a bankia Indignado campaign 83
TOR, the onion router 133
transmission model 45
Tribal Digital Village 35
Tribal Peace 35, 37, 38, 47
Trippi, Joe 16
Trump, Donald 10, 16, 134
Twitter 76

Uber 8
Ulbricht, Ross 50, 59, 61, 63, 71, 125
undersea cables 110, 113

versioning 22

war machine 55
Warrumungu tribe 33
Westphalian model of the state 56
WikiLeaks 6, 31, 49, 51, 69, 70, 111, 115–19, 122, 124–5, 127–8
wiretapping 57

Zapatistas 11
Zapotec 45, 46
Zuckerberg, Mark 28
Zuni 39, 40, 42, 43
Zuni Native American community 39, 40, 42–3, 132

.

.